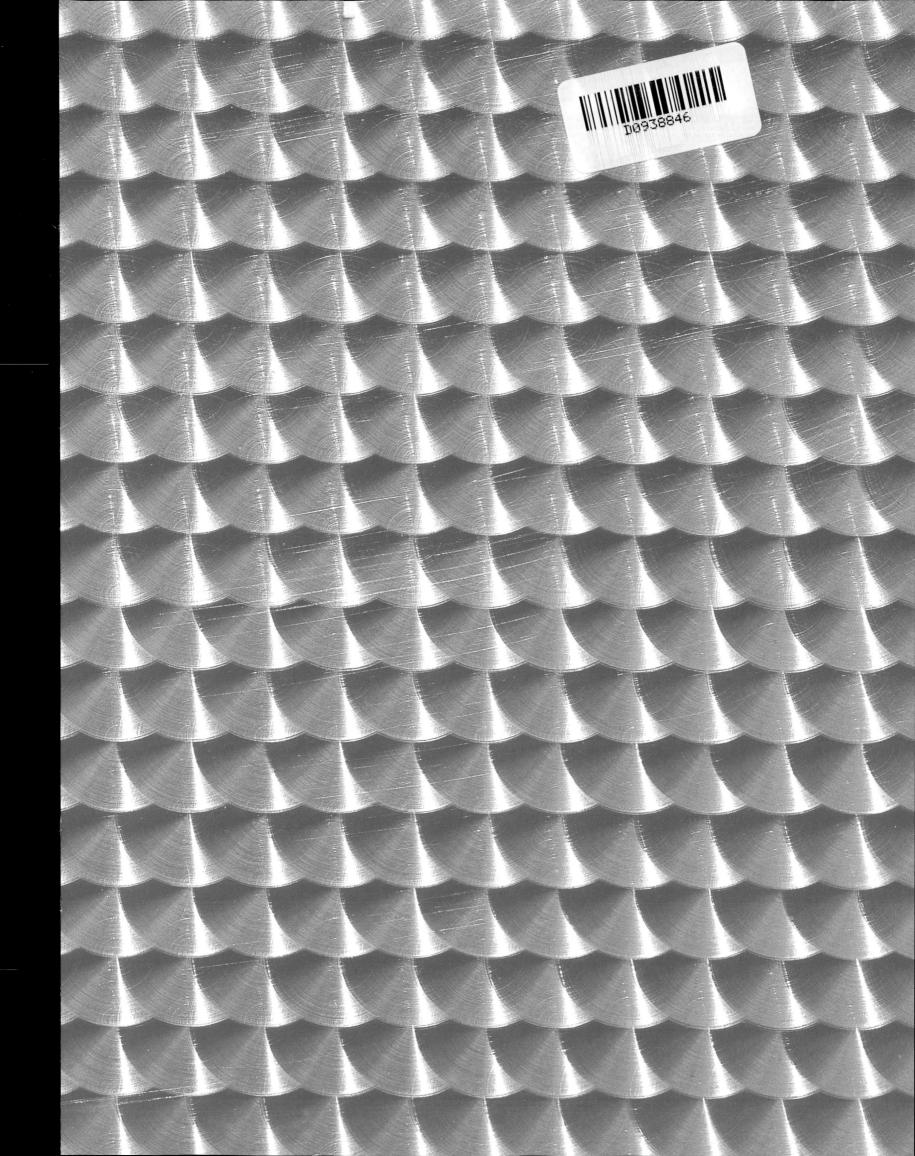

50 YEARS OF ROAD & TRACK
The Art Of The Automobile

BY WM A. MOTTA
AND THE STAFF OF ROAD & TRACK

This edition first published in 1997 by Motorbooks
International Publishers & Wholesalers, 729 Prospect
Avenue, PO Box 1, Osceola, WI 54020 USA

Motorbooks International is a certified trademark,
registered with the United States Patent Office.

The information in this book is true and complete to
the best of our knowledge. All recommendations are
made without any guarantee on the part of the author
or publisher, who also disclaim any liability incurred
in connection with the use of this data or specific
details.

We recognize that some words, model names and
designations, for example, mentioned herein are the
property of the trademark holder. We use them for
identification purposes only. This is not an official
publication.

Motorbooks International books are also available at
discounts in bulk quantity for industrial or sales-
promotional use. For details, write to Special Sales
Manager at the Publisher's address.

Library of Congress Cataloging-in-Publication Data
Available.

ISBN 0-7603-0398-3

Printed in Hong Kong

Front cover painting by Wm A. Motta

Back cover painting of classic BMW 328 by Toby
Nippel. Cartoon of Cyclops at Le Mans by Stan Mott.
Photo of Juan Manuel Fangio and Stirling Moss dueling
in vintage Mercedes and Maserati Grand Prix cars at the
Long Beach GP by John Lamm.

DEDICATED TO
JOHN & ELAINE
TO WHOM WE OWE IT ALL...

CONTENTS

1947/1997

INTRODUCTION

In June, 1947, the first issue of *Road & Track* magazine was offered to the public. Through the first few trying years, publication dates were a bit scattered, but eventually R&T came to be one of the leading car magazines in the world. The goal from the beginning was to publish a magazine for automotive enthusiasts that was authoritative, accurate and ageless.

The graphic presentation that made R&T into something very special came about with the arrival of Hal Crippen as the Art Director in 1959. Hal brought a professional sense of style and elegance to the magazine, a look that separated R&T from all the other automotive publications. And that meant not only excellent photographs, but also a devotion to artwork; drawings, illustrations, paintings, cartoons and even sculptures became vital ingredients in the pages of *Road & Track.*

The book you now hold in your hands is a labor of love. Many people have given their time and energy to create this special celebration of *Road & Track's* 50th Anniversary. The one person who has devoted countless hours, endured sleepless nights and searched out past contributors to the magazine from all around the world is William A. Motta. Bill has worked diligently as the producer and coordinator of this book and has

seen it through to its completion because of his deep love for *Road & Track,* which has been his employer for 37 years. Throughout those years, Bill Motta has done more than any single person to foster the use of the artwork and photography that have made *Road & Track* the exciting magazine it is. Bill spent months combing through 50 years of issues, reducing the number of images that could be included from 2800 to the roughly 450 that would fit within these pages. And he also suggested the various stories that are included, some in their entirety, others in excerpted form.

Many people who are current members of the R&T family pitched in to help move this book from concept to reality. Bill's primary aides in this endeavor were Julie Branch and Stan Griffin, who work on the *Road & Track* Specials staff. Julie and Stan combed files, wrote letters, made phone calls, sent faxes and generally were the glue that bound the project together. Various members of the editorial staff of *Road & Track* contributed their assistance in writing captions, putting words into computers for the layouts and checking and rechecking everything.

We at *Road & Track* are delighted that this book was produced in partnership with our friends at Motorbooks International. We have worked with Motorbooks and its president,

Tim Parker, on many occasions. Our relationship goes back to the earliest days of Motorbooks and its founder, Tom Warth. This cooperation was truly a marriage made in heaven.

If I may presume to speak for everyone who has been involved with *Road & Track* over its first half-century, we see *50 Years of Road & Track* as a wonderful testament to our audience. Throughout the magazine's history, we have all viewed our jobs here as trustees for the readers. This magazine has a uniquely rich heritage in American publishing circles; *Road & Track* created the field of automotive enthusiast publications after World War II and has maintained a level of quality, authority and, most important, integrity unmatched by any other.

This book, *50 Years of Road & Track,* is our opportunity to share with our readers, old and new, past and present, some of the wonderful memories that have brought us to this momentous anniversary.

Every mile a memory.

Thos L. Bryant
Editor-in-Chief
Road & Track

Note: If you are one of the few people we were unable to reach whose work appears in this book, please contact Bill Motta at Road & Track, *1499 Monrovia Ave., Newport Beach, Calif. 92663.*

LOOKING BACK

Reflections on the early days at R&T

By John R. Bond

John R. Bond assumed control of Road & Track *in 1952 and over a period of more than 20 years he and his wife, Elaine, transformed a small, economically pinched automotive magazine into what it is today. Among his many accomplishments, John pioneered the authoritative road testing of cars that has long been the foundation of R&T. The contributions John made to the craft of automotive journalism over the years are without parallel and for our 30th Anniversary in 1977 we asked him to recount some of his most memorable moments.*

T aking over a faltering magazine was and still is a high-risk venture or, in plain language, a gamble. I still think gambling is a sin but that's where we were in November 1952. Not only that, but neither Elaine nor I had any experience whatsoever in the publishing business, a violation of my own theory that anyone going into any business should start at the bottom and learn every facet of the operation. We started at the top and learned fast—we had to!

Looking back on the years of learning, there were some bitter pills, but there were also interesting problems and a sense of being on the right track. Elaine and I liked cars too, which is rather pertinent to the story of the magazine.

■ It's 1952 and the *Road and Track* staff—shown here are Editor Oliver Billingsley (left) and Associate Editor Samuel Weill Jr. (center) with Marian Kaplen and Suzie Fujikawa—worked in a cozy office in Glendale, California.

In those early days, just as today, every *Road & Track* reader had his or her own ideas as to what R&T should or should not be. (We listened.) We talked with printers, distributors, advertising people, writers, other publishers. (We listened.) There were people like engineers, public relations men, plant managers and top auto executives. We visited almost every automobile plant in the U.S. and Europe. *Always* we listened.

In the early years I paid little attention to the business side because I didn't have time. Elaine started as Advertising Director in mid-1953 and relieved me of all the business and financial management problems. All I ever did in this area was ask once a month what our bank balance was after all the bills were paid. She also helped me do the road tests when no else was available. It was always more fun when she went along, except for one day when we returned from testing earlier than expected. It was noon on a Friday and we found the office closed and locked, the rest of the staff having given themselves the afternoon off! It rather spoiled what had been a thrilling morning drive, sweeping around the curves in hilly country on a beautiful day. The car, by the way, was the new MG TF with the 1500 engine.

Early Days & Early Editors

B efore describing some of the more entertaining road tests, I would like to relate, or confess, a few incidents never told before. When we took over, we had a staff of six, 3000 subscribers and newsstand sales were 50,000–70,000 copies per month. One of the staffers we inherited was Bob Dearborn, who was the Editor. His pay was a stupendous $50 per week, but his wife worked to help out. Bob was tremendous in terms of energy, enthusiasm and all-around ability. He and I did most of the road tests, despite his weight of more than 250 lb. But he wasn't too knowledgeable about cars and sometime before we started he bought a 2½-liter Riley. On a run up to the first Pebble Beach race he demonstrated the 90-mph capability of the car for his passengers, and the long-stroke engine blew up. Later he purchased a Rover and wrote the road test in extremely glowing terms. It was a very good car but hardly comparable to a Rolls-Royce. Shortly after we arrived on the scene, I got a call one Sunday. It seems Bob had heard that

rice poured slowly into the carburetor would clean out the carbon. So Elaine and I drove over to his home and listened to the engine. It wasn't running at all well and I had to tell him that it probably had some bent valves. Poor Bob, it did!

After Dearborn left we were even worse off for writers. We bought some articles to help out, even though we couldn't pay much, from people like Roger Huntington (Allan Hunt for us), Griffith Borgeson and many others. I wrote articles too, under other names (Jack Corbin was one), and somehow I managed to turn out a book in 1954, *Sports Cars in Action* by "Henry Holt." We used the money to buy a new VW and make a small down payment on a modest home.

As the years went by, so did many editors. I was pretty hard to satisfy, so I'm told. But in any case there were several who were a tremendous help, but I'll mention only one, Charles Gillet.

One day in 1955 a tall, handsome young man walked into our office with a copy of R&T in his hand. Elaine's office was up front, next to the tiny reception room, so she talked to him first. Every editorial page of Gillet's copy of the magazine was well sprinkled with red marks—errors in punctuation, grammar and even spelling. Elaine called me in and the three of us went to lunch in our VW. (Mr. Gillet's car was a brand new Chrysler-Allard K-3.)

We came back from lunch with a new editor and fired the one we had. Charles was very, very good. One of his goals was to produce a perfect issue, i.e., no typographical errors. All three of us did the proofreading of every page, but somehow the Linotype operator always seemed to hold the winning hand. We would make a correction and he would make two errors, right up to press time. Charles was one of the best, but he left us to go back to Baltimore and build a new VW dealership—40 West Motors. It was and is very successful.

The Cornerstone: Integrity

F rom the beginning there was always a battle over questionable advertising. We wouldn't accept it and the potential advertisers sometimes got very angry, even threatening to sue us. Especially so when we ran editorial comments on the bad products.

PHOTO BY JERRY CHESEBOUGH

Water injection devices were early examples of these kinds of problems. Most of them were not properly engineered, and the claims were totally ridiculous. We wrote that the only good one was the Thompson Vita-Meter. It was never advertised in R&T and manufacture ceased around 1960. However, a very similar injection system was standard (and necessary) on the turbocharged Oldsmobile Jetfire of 1964.

There were others: like Cop-Si-Loy for your brakes, pep pills, a $5 engine overhaul kit in a tube, battery additives, ionization cells for the fuel-feed line, electro-jet sparkplugs and anti-skid control bars. These last, I wrote, were equivalent to turning a bowling ball loose in the trunk! Unfortunately, an occasional questionable ad would slip in because no one saw the copy until it was printed.

We wrote strongly about Ralph Nader's campaign against the Chevrolet Corvair. Later when he attacked VW (see R&T, April 1972), we were more affluent and called a news conference in New York to refute Nader's claims. We got good press but the TV part was a bust because one of Nader's representatives butted in and ranted and raved. …

Road Testing Memories

Beginning in November 1952, I concentrated on making the road tests better. Now most people think this would be the most fun of all, and it was at times. We laid out a carefully measured ¼-mile on a 6-mile straight and level road in the California desert near Mecca. At night we could see car lights for miles from either direction. We erected our own reflector stakes at each end of the ¼-mile section.

The actual testing usually started around midnight, after dinner in nearby Indio. With luck we would be through (with one car) in two or three hours. Then a few hours' sleep in our favorite motel and the 2-hour drive back to the office by midmorning.

We had occasional encounters with the law, such as the night we were testing one of John Von Neumann's Porsches. We were stopped by a deputy sheriff for questioning, but all he said was, "You guys are moving pretty fast back and forth out here; better slow it down." He was nice about it though and said his primary job was "looking for wetbacks."

I guess the most uncomfortable incident was one of the first times we had two cars to test and parked both quite close to a reflector for a midnight conference. The cars were both quite new, an Allard Palm Beach owned by Charles Conn and a Sunbeam Alpine owned by Vilém B. Haan. As we stood there we heard the roar of a speeding car coming toward us. We weren't concerned until the car suddenly braked, parked right behind us, and on

came the red light. The lawman's first words were, "These cars are stolen." He didn't believe our testing story at all (we didn't dare say we were about to clock performances), so he called the station in Indio and asked them to check out the license plate numbers with the motor vehicle department. He told us the the DMV had no record of the license numbers. (The cars were that new and they had not been reported stolen.) We were then interrogated individually in the back of the patrol car. After what seemed like an hour, the deputy still wasn't satisfied and indicated we should drive to Indio, with him following. I suddenly remembered our favorite motel and the name of the lady who owned it. So he called her. We didn't hear what was said but he said, "Okay, I guess you're okay; go on." When we got to the motel much later we asked about the conversation. She said, "Oh, I told the officer you were okay, had reservations for that night and stayed here often. I also told him you're racers!"

Another unforgettable test was the Mercedes-Benz 300SL Gullwing. I, of course, wanted to be the first to publish a road test on this exciting new car. The time arrived and I drove from the Los Angeles area to Mecca. The car at this time was available only with a wobble stick but this was no problem except that the gears sounded like they were straight cut, not helical. Out along the freeway near Pomona, I let it out to 120 mph for a burst and, frankly, I didn't like it. The steering felt extraordinarily quick and overly sensitive. Actually, it was scary, and I was very careful from then on.

A test that fizzled badly was a Dyna Panhard roadster that had been doing well in SCCA class racing. It was supplied by a dealer (Bill Devin) and arrived on a trailer. He drove it off the trailer, warmed it up and I climbed in

with the stopwatches. On the first speedometer check run (at 30 mph) the engine seized. Poor Bill's mechanics had forgotten to put oil in the crankcase! I guess the Panhard was jinxed. We set up another test later on the 4-door sedan and one of the dealer's salesmen rolled it the day before the test!

In all we did about 300 road tests in the period from 1952 to 1965. At that point I gave up the job. We tested a lot of interesting cars and there were many other incidents, like trying to get acceleration figures for a new Rover 3000 on a 4-lane highway on Long Island, or driving off and leaving our test equipment on a sidewalk in San Francisco (we recovered it; nobody knew what it was). But you get the idea. …

Conclusion

My life's dream as a young engineer was to someday be the chief engineer for a major carmaker, and I suppose I must have been talking about that with Elaine several years ago when she said, "But, John, they all listen to you now." It's very satisfying to feel that we have participated in something so worthwhile, namely making and keeping R&T the best automotive magazine we could. It has been a good life.

■ John and Elaine Bond with daughter Lee do a parody of a Chas. Addams cartoon, "Building a Special," published by the SCCA magazine. Below, the Bonds up top and Dean Batchelor at Road America, Elkhart Lake, Wisconsin, in 1956, with R&T's DKW Pressmobile.

PHOTO BY LEO P. CUMMINGS

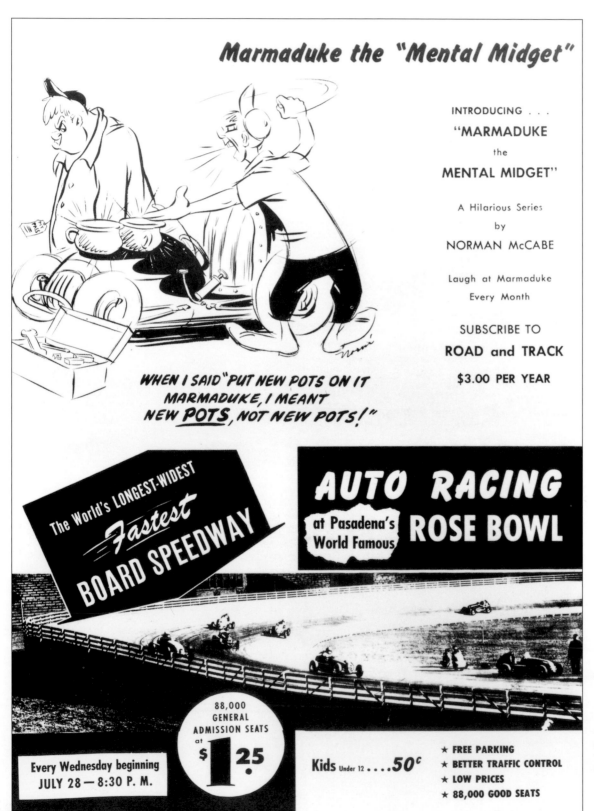

NORMAN McCABE

August 1948

Marmaduke's Pots

There was good jargon to be acquired, and Marmaduke the "Mental Midget" learned it along with the rest of us.

EDWIN H. SEARS

May 1948

Culver City Flugplatz

The year before he finished 12th at Indy, Troy Ruttman already knew a thing or two about piloting a race car; here he is in the A.J. Walker Offy on the road race course at Culver City Speedway in California. And we mean "piloting."

NOT CITED

August 1948

Rose Bowl Board Track

Some of America's earliest racetracks were board-surfaced. And as late as the Forties, this was a fine way to bring racing into an existing venue, even one as traditional as the Rose Bowl.

NOT CITED

March 1950

Clark Gable's Jaguar XK-120

Movie great Clark Gable evidently felt as assured with his cars as he did on the sound stage (but do you suppose he *really* was the author of this?). Others in the series of "Favorite Sports Cars" included a Jaguar 100 championed by Johnny von Ncumann and a 2.3 short-chassis Alfa Romeo owned by reader Secondo Giusti, who later shipped the car east and raced it at Bridgehampton.

MY FAVORITE SPORTS CAR

NO. 3 of a Series

By Clark Gable

I'm generally a man of few words (especially written words) but when requested that I say something about my new Jaguar XK-120 I must confess I felt like trying to outdo Webster. To call the XK "My Favorite Sports Car" is putting it mildly.

I've always been a bug on cars, especially fast ones. From Duesenbergs to and thru hopped-up popular makes, I've owned and/or driven most of them. Many were fast but hard to handle on the turns; some lacked the acceleration that one feels should accompany speed; others were uncomfortable, uneasy, cumbersome, or otherwise undesirable from one standpoint or another. The XK has, so far as I've encountered, none of these drawbacks.

When the 120 was first announced, I was driving a Mark IV Jaguar so I already knew what the name implied. The general appearance and specifications of the car were enough to make me want it like a child wants candy. I wasn't alone in wanting an XK-120, but I was fortunate to be among the early birds in becoming an owner.

As this was shortly after the car had set a world record of over 132 miles per hour for stock production cars, I lost no time in seeing just what mine, which *I KNEW* was strictly stock, would do. So, I decided to try a clocked run at one of the dry lakes here in Southern California. To make a long story short, we went through the measured mile course at (the studio will probably cut this out) 124 mph *(the studio didn't—ed.).* Though the run was timed only by stop watch, it satisfied me.

There were no fancy extras, no specials, no preparatory tuning for this run, so I can't go into any of the technological aspects of special cams, manifolds, carburetors, gear ratios, and the like, but I can and will describe what, to my way of thinking, is a masterpiece of design and construction for a production car. The engine is a twin overhead camshaft six-cylinder Jaguar engine of 3442 cc (210 cu. in.) displacement having a bore of 3¼" and a stroke of 4-3/32 inches. The block is of high grade cast iron, the head—aluminum alloy with spherical combustion chambers. Pistons are aluminum with steel connecting rods coupled to a seven main bearing crankshaft. She puts out 160 HP at 5000 RPM on the tach (and will turn 5300 in a pinch) and is vibrationless and noiseless at all speeds. So much for the unit that makes the XK move the way it does.

I can say, without reservation, that the car is the easiest handing vehicle I have maneuvered at any speed or condition. There isn't the slightest feeling of exceptionally high speed one generally has in smaller automobiles—in fact, for a sense of security at high speed I prefer the Jag regardless of size. As for maneuverability, I'll stack the cornering abilities of the XK against anything I've ever driven. I have put her into as many types and kinds of slides as I know without once having the fear or uneasiness I generally have about whether I'm going to come out in one piece or not. Such characteristics can only mean to me that the car is superbly designed as to steering geometry, weight distribution, braking power, suspension (which is torsion bar on the front and semi elliptic leaf on the rear), and chassis rigidity.

Of course, many of you will say that there can't be "a real live dream car"—one that has absolutely no faults or undesirable qualities—and you'll be right. Some of the things I don't particularly like are the 12 volt system, the non-American screw thread system with its odd size nut and bolt heads, and the lack of a provision for cool air in the cockpit. But to get the thrill of real sport motoring a fellow has to make some sacrifices and if these minor items are all that are required in my case I'll gladly make room for them—until some American manufacturer can give me the same performance, comfort, and price.

BUICK PORTHOLES!

It is interesting to note that the new styling sensation of America, the "Ventiport" was first used on the Mille Miglia Cisitalia coupe, built in 1947. (see photo below) On the Italian car, however, their use was more functional than decorative, being used as exits for the exhaust system. Note also the finned rear fenders, another styling first for Cisitalia.

"It looks like rain, Mac, you put up the top while I cork up the fenders!"

Nice feature, you can signal without putting the window down!

TOM MEDLEY

January 1950

Ventiports, Flint and Italian Style

Artist Tom Medley recalls today, "I did these cartoons back when I was at Art Center. Pete Petersen saw them, I went to work at *Hot Rod,* and I was off and running to a life of cars, cars and more cars. Wouldn't have changed it for the world!"

AN AMERICAN SPORTS CAR?
By John R. Bond

Number One of a Series

Before going very far in any discussion of sports cars, it becomes necessary to attempt some sort of a definition. Perhaps the simplest way to differentiate a sports car from the common production type is to say that a true sports car must offer the enthusiastic and discerning motorist something extra in the way of driving pleasure. Thus, a sports car should not only be capable of exceeding stock car performance as regards acceleration, top speed, cruising speed, and braking power, but also incorporate a certain refinement in controllability and general road-worthiness that makes for all-around safety while still giving pleasure to the owner with an abundance of power under perfect control....

NOT CITED

August 1948

Is a Hot Rod a Sports Car?

None other than John R. Bond took on the challenging question of defining the term "sports car." John and his wife, Elaine, went on to transform R&T into a magazine of international stature. The first piece, though, pictured the likes of Bon Navarro, shown here in his Roots-blown Ford V-8 dry lakes roadster.

NOT CITED

August 1948

The Gatso

International rally star Maurice Gastonides lent his name to this bizarre creation, the Gatso. Profiting from a postwar glut of material, it had a lift-off canopy and aircraft-like bodywork of duralumin. Holland's first postwar car, the Gatso was almost its last.

NORMAN McCABE

January 1950
Marmaduke's Overhead Camshafts
Marmaduke the "Mental Midget" was the Nigel Shiftright of his time. A much different time, true, but there's still resonance with this insider/outsider lingo.

F. TURICH

September 1950
Santa Ana Road Races
The blimp hangar is still a familiar bit of scenery not far from the R&T offices and, in fact, this venue was resurrected for vintage racing in 1996. Back in 1950, it was one of the first sports-car races held in the U.S. Entrants included R&T's Bill Quinn who ran 2nd in class in his 1947 Ford and a fellow named P. Hill who did likewise in a Jaguar XK-120. Yes, P. as in Phil.

Marmaduke the "Mental Midget"

By NORMAN McCABE

NOW WOT'S EATING HIM, I WONDER?

ALFALFA ROMEO

Norm
(IDEA BY TOM CARSTENS)

"Look what he did with my CAMS . . . . . my bee-YOO-tiful OVERHEAD cams!!!"

NOT CITED
June 1947
Indy: The Track of the Month
For the first in a series of significant race circuits, we thought it fitting to choose America's most famous one, the Indianapolis Speedway.

DICK TEAGUE

June 1951

A Revived Mercer Raceabout

For our June 1951 cover, car designer Dick Teague offered his views on updating the Mercer Raceabout, considered among the last of the genuine American sports cars.

LOUIS KIMZEY

March 1951

Hillman Minx Data Panel

This began a tradition of technical art in data panels that continues to Bill Dobson's work of today.

JERRY CHESEBROUGH

August 1951

Phil Hill's 2.9 Alfa at Pebble Beach

Color photography within R&T was a long way off. But this character study of Phil's Alfa Romeo 2900 roaring through the pines of Monterey displays unmistakable artistry.

NOT CITED

October 1951

Rita Hayworth's Alfa

The Beautiful People Drive Beautiful Cars: Glamour queen Rita Hayworth.

NOT CITED

December 1951

Young Donald Campbell

Future speed-record holder Donald Campbell peers from his father's Bluebird land-speed-record car.

PUBLIFOTO

January 1952

Juan Manuel Fangio's First Championship

Capturing his first of five World Driving Championships, Juan Manuel Fangio finished well—albeit didn't absolutely dominate—in five of the seven European Grands Prix. The Indy 500 was also part of the series.

RALPH POOLE

September 1952

Ascari's Ferrari at Indy

The 1952 Indianapolis 500 had a factory entry from Scuderia Ferrari driven by Alberto Ascari; he was running 7th when a wheel hub failed. Three other Ferraris and a Maserati 8CL took part in qualifying.

NOT CITED

November 1952

Porsche 356-4

Amazingly enough, two basic models—this 356 and the subsequent 911—characterize Porsche history and heritage over four decades. This issue marked the first with a Porsche cover subject, one of many to come.

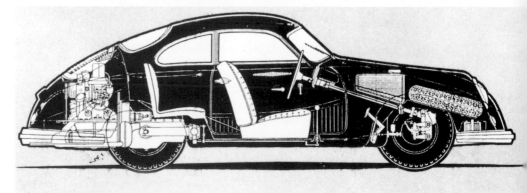

CERA FOTO SERVICES
April 1952
Il Maestro's Alfa
Along with Juan Manuel Fangio
shown here, other driving greats
like Jean Pierre Wimille, Luigi Fagioli
and Dr. Giuseppe Farina demon-
strated the prowess of Alfa's supercharged 1499-cc Type 158-159.

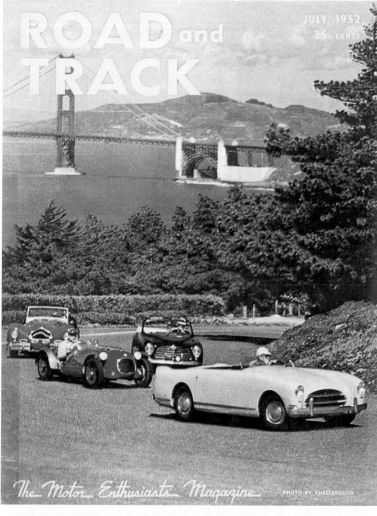

JERRY CHESEBROUGH
July 1952
Golden Gate Road Race
Our cover subject was
a most astounding
venue for a road race:
through Golden Gate
Park, a mere 20 blocks
from the heart of San
Francisco. That's the
Golden Gate Bridge
in the background.

RALPH POOLE
July 1952
Kids and the Crosley
It wasn't easy being the
smallest car on the block.
Nor was it straightforward
for a magazine to foster
small fuel-efficient cars
at a time when Detroit
was just getting into
bigger-is-better.

BERNARD CAHIER
December 1953
Gonzalez' Maserati at Spa
Froilán Gonzalez leads the pack up the hill from the start of the Belgian GP. His wonderfully exuberant driving style was to snap the throttle linkage before long.

NOT CITED
August 1953
First Chevrolet Corvette
With an expected volume of 3000 cars, the Corvette made its debut with 6-cylinder power and automatic transmission. Before long, though, Zora Arkus-Duntov would get involved...

JERRY CHESEBROUGH
January 1953
The Original Watkins Glen
Our caption at the time said it all: "It is not certain that Watkins Glen will play host to road racing next year. The course is rough, lacks proper escape roads, and is too narrow in places."

JERRY CHESEBROUGH
June 1953
Austin-Healey 100
That's Donald Healey at left chatting with R&T's John Bond about the first Austin-Healey 100 to arrive in California. Bond noted that Healey had "a keen appreciation of what we like and, more important, of what we will buy." Indeed.

BILL JENKS
July 1953
Humber Super Snipe
Ever wonder where all those good car names went? The Humber Super Snipe was the Lexus LS 400 of its day, "a well bred, silent touring car."

ROAD & TRACK

June, 1954 LIBRARY COPY 35c the copy

CORVETTE Complete road test / Engineering report • **MG-V8-60 CONVERSION**

THEO PAGE

November 1954
MG EX-179
This record-setting MG special reached 153.69 mph at Bonneville. With its endurance engine fitted, it ran 6 hours at 121.63 mph and 12 hours at 120.87.

HENRY GURR

July 1954
Le Mans Prediction
Gurr foresaw a real duel at Le Mans between the Jaguar D-Type and Lancia. He got it half-right.

NOT CITED

June 1954
Chevrolet Corvette Road Test
Our cover subject goes through its inaugural road test: 0–60 mph, 11.0 sec.; top speed, 107.1 mph.

HENRY GURR

April 1954
The Private War Against Sports Cars
This essay explored subtle undercurrents of social disapproval about high-profile motoring.

ROAD & TRACK

July, 1954 35c the copy

TWO ROAD TESTS: AUSTIN-HEALEY / ALLARD P.B. • **GENEVA SHOW**

NOT CITED

November 1955
Mercedes Benz Pitstop, 1937

A historical piece, "Reflections on Racing" offered the views of Mercedes-Benz at a time when its sports and GP cars were all-conquering.

RON HILL

February 1955
Cover

Snowflakes frame Ron's conception of how a Bugatti Royale coupe might have looked, had Le Patron ever wished to create a sports version of his "golden bug." Mr. Hill is now chairman of the transportation design department of the Art Center College of Design in Pasadena, California.

WARREN C. WHITE

September 1955
Le Mans 1955 Tragedy

An assemblage based on the French Tricolor was our cover theme, serving as a memorial to the 83 people killed in a horrific Le Mans tragedy in which a race car crashed into the crowd.

CARLYLE BLACKWELL

July 1955
Ferrari 2.9 in U.S. Livery

For a long time, paint schemes identified the nationality of race cars, U.S. colors being white with a blue stripe. This lovely Ferrari owed its competition coupe bodywork to Farina; the lady was very attractive as well.

NOT CITED

November 1955
MGA

The MGA appeared as a prototype entry at Le Mans, but later in the year it was introduced as successor to the TF. Such an important new sports car clearly deserved an R&T cover, appropriately framed by the MG octagon.

R.H. GURR

February 1955

Modern Classic Sports Car

John Bond set out a series of Sports Car Design essays. Here in No. 18, he formulated plans for a latter-day Duesenberg, and artist Gurr translated these ideas into handsome artwork.

RALPH POOLE

September 1955

Disneyland "Autopia"

R.H. (Henry) Gurr, the designer of the famous amusement park cars, gives a first ride to a passenger reported to be a very young Strother MacMinn, who is one of the most respected teachers and designers of the last 50 years.

NOT CITED

August 1955

Bosley Special

Richard W. Bosley of Mentor, Ohio, designed and built this fiberglass-bodied, Chrysler V-8 sports car over a period of several years. What's more, this car was to return to R&T almost 40 years later in its September 1994 Salon feature.

ROAD & TRACK

December 1956

35c the copy

G. P. of Europe

Facel Vega

Kombi vs. Karavan

Salon

RALPH POOLE

March 1956

Bugatti Type 38

Ralph Poole photographed many wonderful cars for our Salon series. Few, though, had a history as bizarre as this Type 38: bodywork by Murphy of Pasadena, 124 mph at Muroc Dry Lake, used by a movie studio, once owned by a high school lad named Phil Hill.

CARLYLE BLACKWELL

December 1956

Christmas Ferrari

The closest photographer Carlyle Blackwell could come to a red sleigh for St. Nick is this 3.5-liter Ferrari. The scene is a quiet village on Christmas Eve (on Twentieth Century-Fox's back lot), but if the kiddies are still awake, it's not the sound of sleigh bells they'll be hearing...

GLEN EMBREE

February 1956

High-fashion Ferrari

A high-fashion theme cover features a 4.5-liter Pinin Farina-bodied Ferrari, a nattily dressed driver and yet another stylish woman.

PHILIP TRACHTMAN

May 1956

Carhop-ready MG

We knew we were driving cars that had special characteristics, even to a novel use for the classic fold-down windscreen.

NOT CITED

April 1956

General Motors Motorama

GM's Buick Centurion show car with rearview TV and 325-bhp V-8.

ROAD & TRACK

February 1956

35c the copy

ROADTESTS | **ARNOLT-BRISTOL FORD 'STOCK-CAR'** • **LONDON SHOW**

Searching for a Vision
1957-1966

JOE PARKHURST

July 1957
Jaguar XK-SS

"Watch me blow off that funny little car," says Chromobile driver. The XK-SS, of course, was the road-going version of Jaguar's amazing D-Type. Artist Parkhurst later founded our sister publication, *Cycle World*.

R.H. GURR

November 1957
Beauty and the Beetle

"Much speculation existed in the mid-late Fifties as to what a "real" VW should look like. Unfortunately, I went for the full GM cliché. Time has now taught us that you don't mess with functional purity."

STAN MOTT

March 1957
Beyond Belief

"The Cyclops II was created in retaliation to the 1958 Buick Riviera. It was a broadside against Detroit decadence, a cry for freedom, an exercise in simple-mindedness; bend a rectangular piece of metal into a 'U', punch out a windshield and backlight, fit them in as sides, add details, and *voilá!* a Cyclops II. Robert Cumberford wrote and I illustrated the first Cyclops article, 'Beyond Belief,' March 1957. Cyclops was an instant success. Using the article's drawings as a guide, enthusiasts built them at home and raced them at Cumberland, Maryland. One enthusiast described Cyclops as 'the Charlie Chaplin of automobiles, the underdog who always wins.' It always did win. That first article was followed by 22 Cyclops features over the next 35 years, totaling 152 drawings and over 50,100 words. They invariably described how the mini machine won real and imagined world-class races and rallies. For non-believers, there is a Cyclops II parked in the lobby of the *Road & Track* editorial office.

"The first shipment was herded down to the Italian coast and lashed together as an aircraft carrier-like ship. One of the car's engines was hooked up to a propeller and powered it to America."

RUSSELL BROCKBANK

March 1958
Klaxon Spray
Cartoons by Brockbank delight one and all with whimsical happenings. His first appearance in R&T came in this review of *The Brockbank Omnibus,* a collection originally appearing in *Punch.*

NOT CITED

January 1958
MG Montlhéry
A controversial cover: Its vertical format optimized the automotive shape, but angered some; yet another pretty face prompted more than a few readers to write indignantly about their "car magazine" going to the ladies...

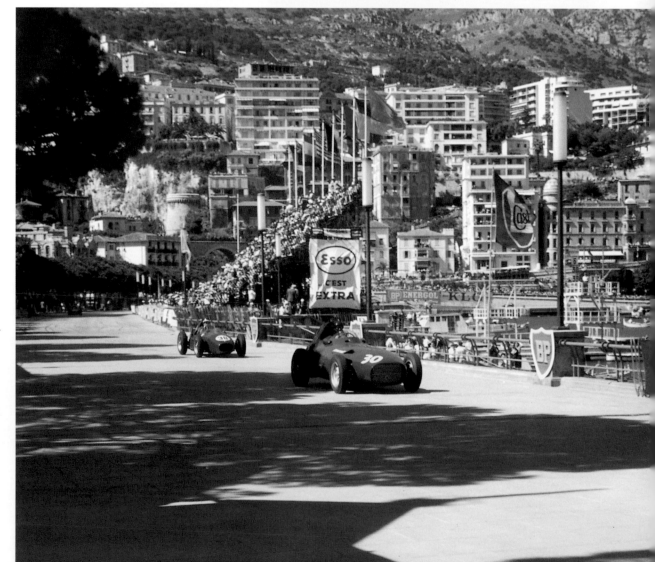

HENRY MANNEY

October 1958
Vanwall and Ferrari at Monaco
Bernard Cahier still handled our Grand Prix coverage, but a talented young man named Henry Manney was over there as well with camera and, before long, with notebook.

STROTHER MacMINN

February 1958

An American Car for Le Mans

In his Sports Car Design No. 41, John Bond proposed a sleek competition coupe especially designed to take U.S. colors to Le Mans.

TOBY NIPPEL

August 1958

Ulster Aston Martin

This was the first of a series of beautiful paintings that Toby did of Salon cars, art that was admired and collected by automotive enthusiasts all over the world. He influenced generations of automotive artists to come.

RAY RICH

October 1958

Hot Air Flow

Ray's illustration and story speculate what a car designed for politicians would look like. The driver must be capable of smiling, shaking hands and downshifting, while throwing his weight around the course.

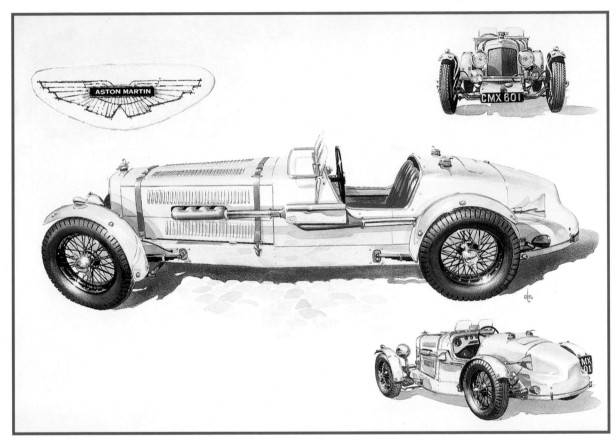

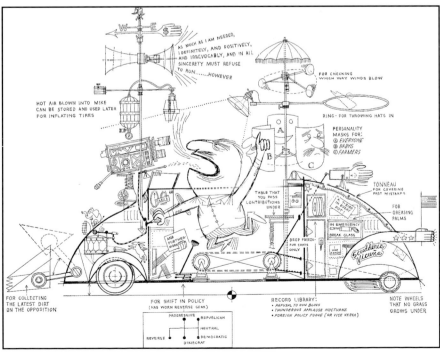

STROTHER MacMINN

November 1958

R&T's 750-cc Car

No. 48 in John Bond's Sports Car Design series, this tidy little package was intended to update the British concept of low-cost, small-displacement racing. Its wedge-shape bodywork covered a wealth of existing hardware.

TOBY NIPPEL

May 1959

MG K-3 Magnette

Upon the introduction of a new and much more civilized Magnette, Toby takes a longing look backward at the romantic K-3.

MARVIN RUBIN

January 1959

Beyond the Fire

Provocative fiction has been an important element of R&T, and it often provided the setting for equally provocative art. Here Marvin Rubin illustrates Charles Beaumont's fable of saber-toothed Buicks, armor-topped Fords and other automotive perils "Beyond the Fire."

MARVIN RUBIN

June 1959

24 Hours to Le Mans

Marvin captures some of the adventure of driving a Cadillac-Allard to Le Mans from an air force base in Germany. The wonderfully whimsical illustration was done in scratch-board.

BOB THATCHER

March 1959

The Thousand-dollar Sports Car

"Quite seriously," wrote John R. Bond, "it can be done." However, this involved buying "a 1949 Ford (which runs) for under $200."

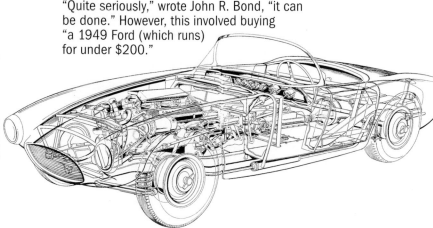

BEST BUYS

One question that seems perennial these days is which country builds the most or best quality into its automobiles. Popular opinion often gives the Germans the nod, but we do not agree at all.

First we must define quality, and this is all but impossible. Most people think of the finish, body panel fits, trim details, etc. The manufacturing department thinks of close tolerances, surface finish on machined parts, heat treatments and the like. The engineer thinks of design excellence and material choice, among other things. However, the end result should be a car that is pleasing to the customer and one that covers the most miles for the lowest upkeep cost.

In our opinion, there is no appreciable difference in the overall quality of cars, whether they come from the U.S., France, Germany, England, Italy or Sweden. There are a few bad ones, but they are soon found out. The companies either make corrections or go out of business. That's one reason so many makes have disappeared.

Selecting a list of top-grade quality-built cars is a little easier, though arbitrary. Some may surprise our readers, others will not. We chose these cars as being the best made in the world and of approximately equal quality, making some allowance for first cost in terms of value per dollar.

1. Rolls-Royce and Bentley, England
2. Mercedes-Benz, Germany
3. Lancia, Italy
4. Rover, England
5. BMW, Germany
6. Peugeot, France
7. Cadillac, U.S.

JOHN BOND

September 1959
Best Buys
John Bond offered this somewhat iconoclastic listing of top-grade, high-quality cars long before the trivialization of lists, both automotive and otherwise, done every which way.

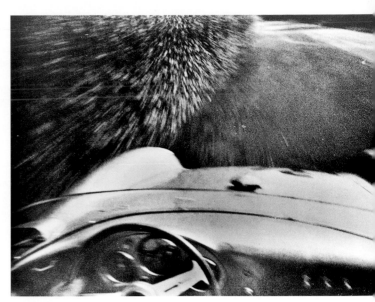

JULIUS WEITMANN

April 1959
The Racing Driver
This is one of the finest and earliest photos to appear in R&T that truly captures the essence of speed from a moving race car. The photo illustrated perfectly an excerpt from Denis Jenkinson's book, subtitled *"The theory and practice of fast driving."*

STROTHER MacMINN AND SYDNEY MEAD

May 1959
The R&T Small Car
John Bond and other R&T staff members provided the packaging constraints: Come up with a small-car design that's practical, functional and most definitely not dumpy.

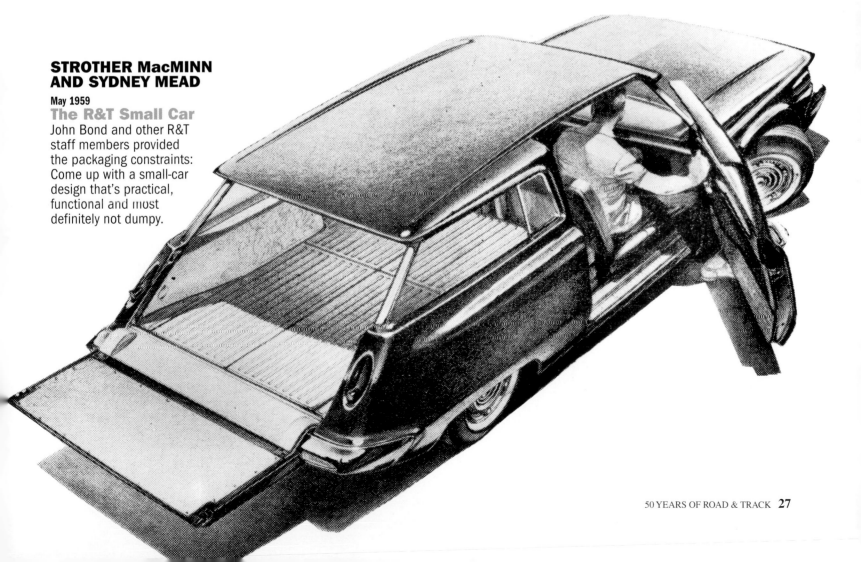

WILLIAM CLAXTON
November 1959
Scarab Formula 1
Hopes were high for Lance Reventlow's radically crafted Scarab, designed to bring F1 laurels to this side of the Atlantic. Alas, it was not to be.

BERNARD CAHIER
November 1959
Avus Grand Prix
The German GP that year was held at Berlin's Avus circuit that Cahier thought outdated and dangerous, its 43-degree banking indifferently paved in brick.

TOBY NIPPEL
August 1959
Blower Bentley
Could there ever be an automobile more gloriously British than a Blower Bentley?

NOT CITED

January 1960
Canadian Zar Car
Where's the Dutch Gatso when we need it?

WM A. MOTTA

July 1960
Grand Prix Ferrari
Our own Art Editor, and indeed the guiding force of this very book, first appeared in the pages of R&T several years before he did this carefully drafted Ferrari, one of the last of the front-engine Grand Prix cars.

JON DAHLSTROM

June 1960
Miscellaneous Ramblings
This is the first of many delightful illustrations to come from the pen and brush of one of the finest and most original of our long list of exceptional artists.

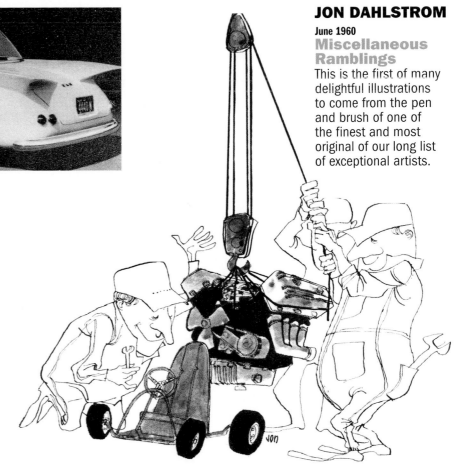

RALPH POOLE

August 1960
Sports Car
Design Realized
John Bond's American
Car for Le Mans was
translated into hardware
by three Southern
California enthusiasts.

GENE HOLTAN

August 1960
Visit to a Hairy Planet
In this Roger Proulx fantasy,
Captain Xendl wisely persuades
the Administrator and his Cabinet
that Earthlings and their motor-
sports aren't to be trifled with.
Gene Holtan's art sets the mood.

STAN MOTT

August 1960
Les 24 Heures du Cyclopes II
The Cyclops racing team cuts it close
in the Esses for a 1, 2, 3 win in the
1964 24 Heures du Mans!

JON DAHLSTROM
September 1960
"Have a Car Waiting"
Kelly Rollins shares the joys and
tribulations of overseas delivery.
Jon illustrates how it should be—but isn't.

RUSSELL BROCKBANK
August 1960
Mini Incident
A great deal resides in the facial
expressions of Brockbank folk,
human and otherwise; this cartoon
was incorporated into John Bond's
Miscellaneous Ramblings column.

WM A. MOTTA
May 1960
Rodger Ward
A fine character study of USAC
driver Rodger Ward by our talented
Art Editor, back at a time in his
career when he signed his
works B. Motta.

Ron Flockhart and Jaguar on the Mulsanne Straight, LeMans, 1957   Painting by Roy Nockolds

LE MANS
Les 24 Heures du Spectateur

STORY AND PHOTOS BY JOSEPH C. PARKHURST

ROY NOCKOLDS

July 1960
Le Mans
Roy captures the serenity of speed at night with the headlights glaring off the haze on the Mulsanne Straight. It was the lead illustration for a story by Joe Parkhurst.

WM A. MOTTA

January 1960
Richie Ginther
A California kid with a knack for things mechanical, Richie Ginther went on to give Honda its first Grand Prix win, Mexico 1965.

TOBY NIPPEL

February 1960
Bugatti Type 51-A
He was Italian by birth
and chose to live in
Alsace, but the cars of
Ettore Bugatti clearly
wear French Racing
Blue with pride.

R&T PS

May 1961   Volume 12   No. 9

PETE BIRO PHOTO

Ol' Peter Rabbit may be at a slight disadvantage, displacement-wise, but he has a good line through the corner and more maneuverability than his four-wheeled competitors—plus almost unmatched acceleration—so he may yet catch his competition on the next lap.

WM A. MOTTA
November 1961
Salon, MG TC
Bill says: "This was the first MG TC that I had painted and it started a love affair with these cars that has endured to this day."

PETE BIRO
May 1961
Peter Rabbit Clips the Apex
Pete Biro used a 300-mm Kilfit lens on an Exacta 35-mm camera to catch this long-eared 4x4 mixing it up with the others at Vacaville, California.

MARVIN RUBIN
December 1961
Rolls-Royce Leather
"No Chauffeur Required," by Arthur W. Ploscowe, details the pleasures of Rolls-Royce ownership.

Enough leather to make 128 pairs of shoes.

MARVIN RUBIN

January 1961
Stiff Upper Lip
We learned very proper usage from Harry Roberts' "The Compleat Spectator."

KEN PARKER

February 1961
For Sale Spin
This Austin-Healey Sprite is dually on the sales block and the hay bale.

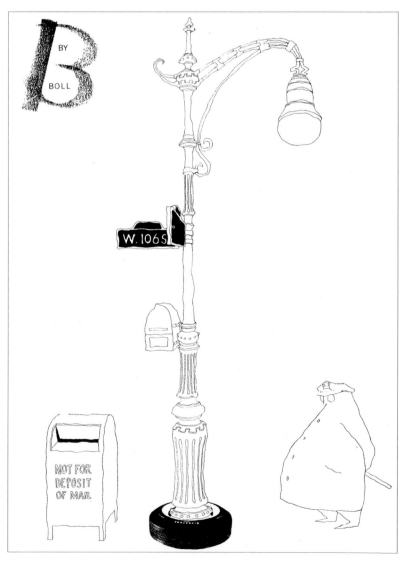

BOLL

April 1961
Tire Lamppost
How did that tire get there? Through the whimsy of Boll, that's how.

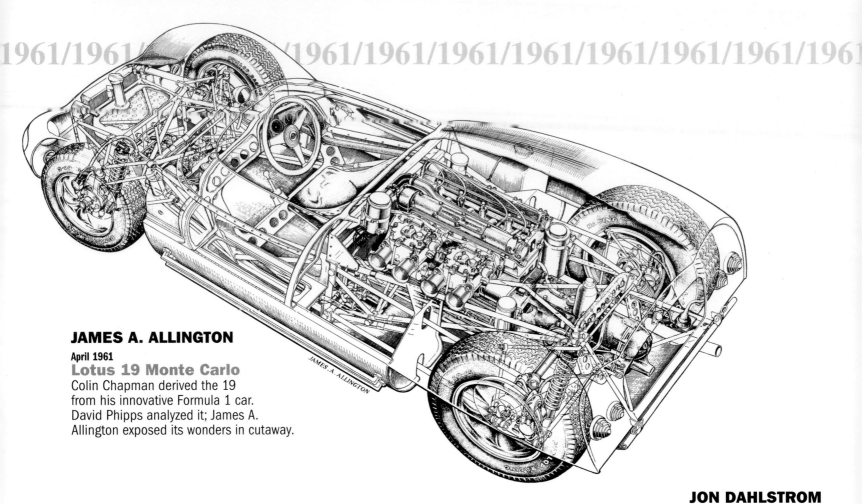

JAMES A. ALLINGTON

April 1961
Lotus 19 Monte Carlo
Colin Chapman derived the 19 from his innovative Formula 1 car. David Phipps analyzed it; James A. Allington exposed its wonders in cutaway.

BOB THATCHER

May 1961
Lancia/Ferrari D-50
Among the "Successes & Failures" recounted, this 1956 Formula 1 car evolved from Lancia difficulties and Ferrari strengths.

JON DAHLSTROM

July 1961
Classified Information
Len Prokine steered us through the definitions of "One of a Kind" (and for good reason), "95% Restored" (but will you ever find the other 5%?) and other bits of classified information.

WM A. MOTTA

March 1961
Alfred Momo
The Carl Haas of his era in American sports-car racing.

TOBY NIPPEL

May 1961
Alfa Romeo 1750
This lovely Alfa was owned by Phil Hill, who recounts he found it listed in a newspaper ad amid used Edsels and the like.

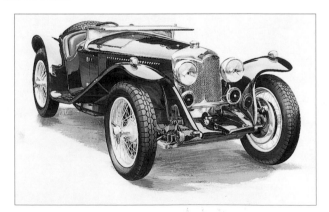

TOBY NIPPEL

July 1961
Riley Nine Imp
Percy Riley's cars, even the sedans, always had a rakish charm. This sporting derivative looks especially so in Toby Nippel's rendition.

TOBY NIPPEL

September 1961
Mercedes-Benz 300SL
The famous Gullwing began as a works racing car in 1952. Today, it's a most sought-after classic.

ALLAN THOMAS
February 1961
Pacific GP Pit Action
Laguna Seca was the venue for a
Pacific Grand Prix sports-car race.
Allan Thomas' woodcut set the mood.

KURT WORNER
February 1961
Fangio Comforts Gonzalez
Kurt Wörner captures the tragic element of
motorsports here, when after hearing news of
the death of compatriot Onofre Marimon,
Fangio comforts Froilán Gonzalez.

SAN FRANCISCO CABLE CAR
Story by Tony Hogg

The ultimate town car, with instant acceleration, fantastic wear index, all-weather traction, phenomenal passenger capacity, and an unmatched degree of customer loyalty.

A common illusion among readers of automobile magazines is that the life of the road tester is one long round of novelty and excitement. Actually, this is far from the truth, because his days are almost entirely occupied in trying to accurately assess the performance and handling qualities of such mundane automobiles as the XK-E Jaguar, the DB-4 Aston Martin (see page 26) and, perhaps, an occasional Ferrari or Scarab. However, the appalling monotony of this work is occasionally relieved by the presentation of a vehicle which, because of its superlative performance and unsurpassed beauty of line, stands head and shoulders above all other machines. One such vehicle, which was offered to us recently for testing, is the San Francisco cable car. …

In an age of conformity, the San Francisco cable car bristles with novel design features. Being upholstered throughout in wood, it can be criticized from the standpoint of passenger comfort, and its maximum speed is low by today's standards, but for sheer simplicity, durability, ease of maintenance and ability to climb hills, it is without peer, and we confidently predict that it will continue to withstand the test of time.

PETE BIRO
April 1962
San Francisco Cable Car
This gripping analysis by Editor-to-be Tony Hogg was our first April Fools' Road Test.

HENRY MANNEY

January 1962
Phil's Pit Signal
At the 1901 Le Mans, the team was giving Phil's teammate the "slow down" signal, but Phil had ideas of his own. Our man Manney was there.

WM A. MOTTA

April 1962
San Francisco Cable Car Data Panel
Everything you ever wanted to know about a cable car, but didn't even know to ask.

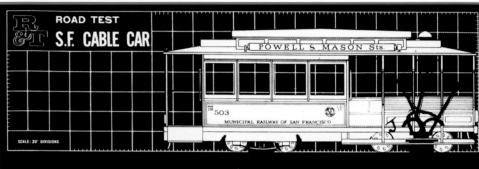

ROAD TEST — S.F. CABLE CAR — POWELL & MASON Sts. — 503 — MUNICIPAL RAILWAY OF SAN FRANCISCO — SCALE: 20" DIVISIONS

DIMENSIONS

Wheelbase, in	194
Tread, f and r	44
Over-all length, in	312
width	90
height	120
equivalent vol, cu ft	1950
Frontal area, sq ft	75
Ground clearance, in	2.3
Steering ratio, o/a	n.a.
turns, lock to lock	n.a.
turning circle, ft	26
Hip room, front	96
Hip room, rear	2x35
Pedal to seat back, max	n.a.
Floor to ground	23.0

CALCULATED DATA

Lb/hp (test wt)	21.8
Cu ft/ton	239
Mph/1000 rpm	13.2
Motor revs/mile	4550
Cable travel, ft/mile	5280
Rpm @ 2500 ft/min	2150
equivalent mph	28.4
R&T wear index	0.00000094

SPECIFICATIONS

List price	n.a.
Curb weight, lb	16,000
Test weight	16,340
distribution, %	50/50
Tire size	20x2
Brake swept area	(see text)
Engine type	electric
	(Fairbanks-Morse)
Displacement, cc	n.a.
cu in	n.a.
Compression ratio	n.a.
Bhp @ rpm	750 @ 720
equivalent mph	9.5
Torque, lb-ft	5460 @ 720
equivalent mph	9.5

GEAR RATIOS

4th (27.0)	27.0
3rd (27.0)	27.0
2nd (27.0)	27.0
1st (27.0)	27.0

SPEEDOMETER ERROR

30 mph (no speedo, no error)	
60 mph	

PERFORMANCE

Top speed (1st), mph	9.5
best timed run	9.5
3rd (720)	9.5
2nd (720)	9.5
1st (720)	9.5

FUEL CONSUMPTION

Normal	560 kw/h

ACCELERATION

0-9.5 mph, sec	1.0
0-40	
0-50	
0-60	
0-70	
0-80	
0-100	
Standing ¼ mile	95.6
speed at end	9.5

TAPLEY DATA

1st, lb/ton @ mph	off scale
2nd	n.a.
3rd	n.a.
Total drag at 60 mph, lb	

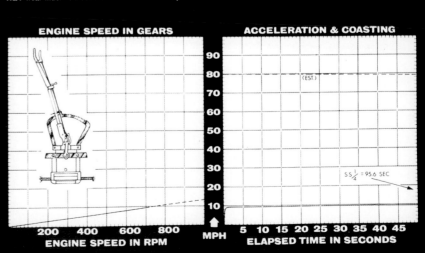

ENGINE SPEED IN GEARS — ACCELERATION & COASTING

(EST.)

SS ¼ = 95.6 SEC

200 400 600 800 — MPH — ENGINE SPEED IN RPM — 5 10 15 20 25 30 35 40 45 — ELAPSED TIME IN SECONDS

JON DAHLSTROM

August 1962

Mad Dogs and Body English

Author Ray Ostergard recognized that motor scooterists
were never truly alone and Jon evidently concurred.

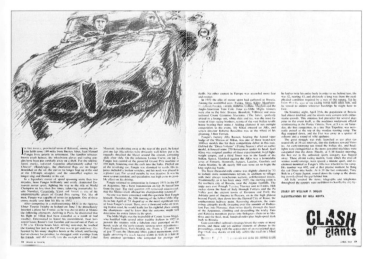

WM A. MOTTA

April 1962

Clash of Giants

Author William F. Nolan recalled
the tortuous 1953 Mille Miglia;
Bill Motta illustrated
the excitement.

GENE GARFINKLE

July 1962

Studebaker Proposal

The Studebaker Avanti made its appearance.
"After Ten Years" offered the opinions of David Ross and
styling views of Gene Garfinkle on what might have been.

HORST BAUMANN

October 1963
$5,000,000 Failure?
Donald Campbell's wife, Tonia, holds his salt shoes as the crew gets his Bluebird land-speed-record car under way at Lake Eyre, Australia.

RUSSELL BROCKBANK

November 1963
Mirror Image
We could always count on Brockbank to see happenings from a unique point of view.

BILL NEALE

June 1963
Sebring Pit Board
This Florida airport circuit has always had atmosphere, caught here in pit-board communication painted by Bill Neale.

HENRY MANNEY

May 1963
Wire Wheel
Manney photographed this symbol of automotive enthusiasm at Turin; it graced our cover story on the New York Auto Show.

Tests: Simca 1000 Sedan & Bertone Coupe ✳ Daytona Report
TOURING NEW ENGLAND   NEW WAVE OF TEXAS RACING TEAMS

MAY 1963
FIFTY CENTS

ROAD & TRACK

THE MOTOR ENTHUSIASTS' MAGAZINE

New York International Auto Show Preview & Guide to the New Cars

TOBY NIPPEL

September 1963
BMW 328
A stylish roadster was the Salon subject accompanying a full history of this Bavarian marque.

JAY VANCE

January 1963
Riverside Spectators
Jack Smith, Los Angeles newspaper columnist, daydreamed about attending his first sports-car race; artist Jay Vance helped the musings along.

HOWARD SHOEMAKER

June 1963
I Love My Wife, But Oh You Car!
Most car enthusiasts can relate to this delightful illustration by one of our longtime artists—who also was a Porsche owner for many years.

RUSSELL BROCKBANK

March 1964
Ilo du Lovant

Together with Henry Manney, Brockbank exposes all—well, almost all—at this Golden Isle of naturalism.

BILL NEALE

January 1964
Jim Clark: 1963 World Champion

Our cover celebrated Jim Clark's (and Lotus') domination of the 1963 Formula 1 season with this handsome collage by Bill Neale.

STAN MOTT

June 1964
East African Safari Cyclops

Crunchcog and Meshingear demonstrate the cornering technique that helped them win the 1964 East African Safari Rally.

An Incompleat Guide to the

ILE DU LEVANT

*Or, where to park your car
while investigating
the bare and the beautiful
of the Golden Isles*

BY HENRY N. MANNEY

ILLUSTRATIONS BY RUSSELL BROCKBANK

A GOOD PERCENTAGE of France's population goes every year to the Cote d'Azur (loosely called Riviera) simply because there is sun. The northern Atlantic beaches, while charming indeed, suffer from an abnormal tidefall, and thus large quantities of mudflat may be exposed most of the day. Furthermore, there tends to be a constant wind and while this is great for sailing or seagulls, it tends to be a little too bracing for lying on the beach. On the other hand, the wine dark Mediterranean suffers little variation in level, what breeze there is comes as more than welcome, and even if the beaches tend to be both over-crowded and rocky, they are at least warm. Also, for the male segment of the population, much better sport than seagull spotting may be indulged in, as the Riviera is the birthplace of France's national costume, the bikini. The sun is there, a tan is smart, why not indulge?

As Europe is an extremely northern continent, sun-worship is much stronger here than in the U.S. At the least feeble ray, large numbers of people are to be seen sitting in the parks with faces upturned. Consequently, there are those for whom even the bikini is an obstacle to full enjoyment of this precious gift and one hears of colonies of *naturistes* all over Europe. I used to have a friend who was a practicing nudist and I must say that they were on a par with vegetarians and other crack groups. They made too much of a Thing about it to be relaxing. Tea dances in the nude may be all very well but when there is a sort of a beadle around

to tap you on the shoulder when impropriety nudges . . . well, who needs it? Consequently, it was with some indifference that I learned, when spending a week or so with my family at Le Lavandou on the Cote d'Azur, that one of the larger islands offshore harbored a thriving resort for naturistes. You know what to expect: fat old men, ancient ladies with spaniels' ears, earnest middle-aged librarians with spectacles and wooden beads, the lot.

The beach at Le Lavandou is sand, not bad at all, but far too cluttered up with people and especially children, who seem to divide their time between throwing buckets at each other and screaming. Consequently, when a really sparkling day came around and I remembered that Loulou le Corsaire, among other wherrymen, ran boats out to the Ile du Levant every hour or so, I collected a clean towel in a string bag and set forth for the docks. The round trip ticket cost 12.50 francs for the 45-min. journey *chez* Loulou and, whereas others may be cheaper, he boasted the largest and most seaworthy-looking boats. A considerable number of passengers came aboard and took their seats on the benches along the sides; they didn't look in the least like sex maniacs, but generally like a cross section of any excursion trip anyplace else in the world, except that there were rather less of the ubiquitous middle-aged American "girls" in tennis hats, bobby sox, and drip-dry skirts. There were children, a baby or two, young couples, (mostly with camping equipment), older people, a sprinkling of single men of all ages, and even a dog. There were also a few remarkably pretty girls

GUNTHER MOLTER

March 1964

Mercedes-Benz W163

Famed motorsports photographer Gunther Mölter captured Hermann Lang at speed in the Mercedes-Benz W163, a marque that, along with Auto Union, overpowered Grand Prix racing in the late Thirties.

GEOFFREY GODDARD

September 1964
A Bizarre Belgian GP
It was right out of Hollywood: Dan Gurney runs out of gas. Jim Clark does likewise on the cool-off lap, only to learn he won the race.

Grand Prix of
BELGIUM
Spa Francorchamps

A vignette from the last lap featuring Dan Gurney and Jim Clark

Gurney runs out of gas near Stavelot and coasts to a stop . . . ➡

. . . to look at his engine and to (hopefully) find a miracle . . .

. . . the two compare notes. The race is officially over . . .

. . . and Clark thinks he's third . . .

. . . so a good laugh is had by both as they see the joke . . .

I won!

. . . both drivers . . .

GEOFF GODDARD PHOTOS

. . . but dejectedly faces the inevitable . . .

. . . Clark stops by on cool-off lap, and runs out of gas.

. . . P.A. says Hill is also out . . .

. . . the loudspeaker announces Clark is first and McLaren second . . .

. . . wait for a ride . . .   *. . . Arundell arrives . . .*   *. . . and carries Clark off piggyback to collect his laurels.*

RICHARD CORSON
November 1964
Bugatti Type 59
An accomplished writer as well as artist, Richard Corson visited Rouen, France, in 1964 and heard "Echoes of Past Thunder" from cars such as Aston Martin, Bentley, the ERA "Remus" and this Bugatti Type 59.

Frankfurt Auto Show & Ten New Mercedes

ROAD&TRACK

DECEMBER 1965   THE MOTOR ENTHUSIAST'S MAGAZINE   3/6 IN ENGLAND   60 CENTS

Jim Clark's Own Account of 500 Victory

BILL NEALE

December 1965

The World Champion, Jim Clark, and his Lotus

This wonderful cover illustration captured the magic of Jim Clark. And inside, we ran a feature by Clark, titled "How I won at Indy," which was reprinted from *Competition News,* Ford of Britain's Motoring Newspaper.

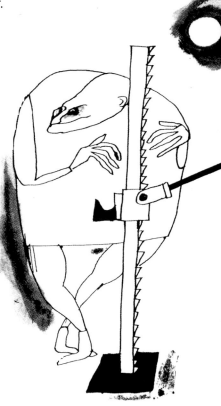

HOWARD SHOEMAKER

February 1965

A Question of Jacks

Haunting art by Shoemaker accompanied a humorous story by Bob Dearborn wondering where all the bumper jacks go when cars are dismantled or sent to wrecking yards.

STAN MOTT

August 1965

The Adventures of Cyclops 007

Stan Mott's wonderful saga of Piero Martini and the Cyclops continued with "The real story of the 49th Targa Florio" in which the 30-cc, olive-oil-burning slot car won the race...sort of.

HORST BAUMANN

November 1965

The New Matadors

Racing photographer Baumann produced stunning images for the R&T book, *The New Matadors,* written by Ken Purdy. The book was a work of art in both stories and photos, and this one was from the page titled "Small sideshows characteristic of Indianapolis."

50

CAMERON A. WARREN
November 1965
PS

"In every traffic jam there's always this guy in the back who thinks he's Stirling Moss."

WM A. MOTTA
December 1965
Salon: Morgan Super Sport

Bill Motta's painting of the 3-wheel Morgan Super Sports was the centerspread of that month's Salon, written by Tony Hogg.

**HOWARD
SHOEMAKER,
JACK SMITH**

July 1966
Weekend Affair
Noted *Los Angeles Times* columnist Jack Smith was an occasional contributor to R&T over many years. In this story, Smith reveals the joy of driving a Citroën for the weekend. Artist Shoemaker captured the whimsy in his illustrations.

WEEKEND AFFAIR

"It is the CADILLAC of France," the Citroën mechanic told me. "You will be very 'appy."

"I hope I'm not too happy," I said. "I'm only taking it out for the weekend. I wouldn't want to fall in love."

It was a new pearl-white DS-21 with upholstery the color of a good red Bordeaux.

"Please to get in," said the Citroën man. "I show you how she work."

We got in. In a moment the whole car rose like a cake. It was adjusting to our avoirdupois, regaining its aplomb, the man explained.

We spun around the block. He briefed me on all the pips, levers, switches, gauges, pedals and cranks, and the knob by which one can raise or lower the chassis—even at 60 miles an hour.

"And the brake, monsieur," he said. "She is on the floor, eh? This little button. Like a champignon. How you say— a mushroom, yes?"...

I drove the Citroën home. I felt like a schoolboy on his first assignation. My performance was not flawless. The DS-21 is not a vulgar wench from Detroit, insensitive to loutishness and stupidity. She must be courted, not forced.

I shifted like a bear. I couldn't find the brake. I kept waving my foot around in the air above it.

"Mushroom," I had to remind myself. "A little mush-room on the floor. Yes?"

I parked in the driveway. My wife came out and walked around the Citroën.

"It's gorgeous," she sighed. "It's so—French!"

"You are a Francophile," I told her....

By the time we hit the Ventura Freeway and headed home I was the Citroën's master. We floated along like two angels on wine-red clouds.

"Gorgeous," my wife said. "Absolutely dreamy."

I felt happy as a bird. I found myself humming. It was a tantalizing tune, but I couldn't quite place it.

"What *is* this?" I asked, humming it again.

"*Mademoiselle de Paris*," she said. "It's French."

"Good Lord!" I thought. "I've been brainwashed!"

"Well, how do you like the Citroën?" the mechanic asked when I took it back.

"Beautiful," I admitted. "But it's a little different from my Dodge—handling, that is."

"Oui," he said. "*Vive la difference!*"

GURNEY-WESLAKE GRAND PRIX ENGINE ANALYSIS

ROAD & TRACK

JUNE 1966   THE MOTOR ENTHUSIASTS' MAGAZINE   3/6 IN ENGLAND   SIXTY CENTS

Eagle T2G – Indianapolis Version

STIRLING MOSS ON THE SAFARI RALLY

WM A. MOTTA

June 1966

Eagle T2G—Indianapolis Version

Dan Gurney's All American Racers' Eagle was the subject of this cover painting. The issue also contained a story on the Gurney-Weslake Grand Prix engine being developed in England.

JON DAHLSTROM

September 1966
So You'd Like to Own a Ferrari
Contributing Artist Dahlstrom captured the sex appeal and potential trials of owning a Ferrari, to illustrate this story by Bill Davis.

WM A. MOTTA

November 1966
Ferry Porsche III
Jerry Sloniger wrote a feature/interview with the 30-year-old chief of Porsche's design studio. Bill Motta illustrated the pragmatic Butzi Porsche surrounded by some of the cars he designed.

LEO BESTGEN

November 1966
Juliette
"After all, she was nothing but a machine, a beautiful machine..." was the closing line of Claude F. Cheinisse's tragic tale of his romance with a car. Bestgen's illustration captures the magic of that story.

CAMERON A. WARREN

July 1966
PS
"Aw, c'mon, Dan—you know Fords don't go 'phrrrrt'!"
Contributing Photographer Cam Warren always seemed
to be in the right place at the right time.

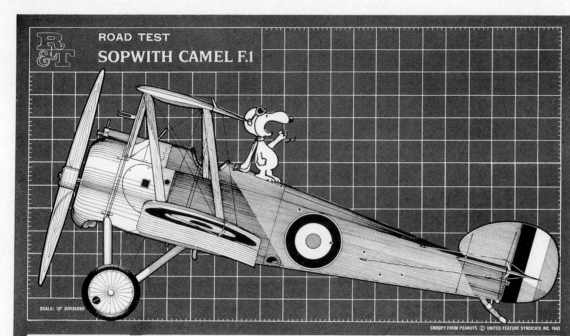

ROAD TEST
SOPWITH CAMEL F.1

SCALE: 10" DIVISIONS

SNOOPY FROM PEANUTS © UNITED FEATURE SYNDICATE INC. 1965

ENGINE

Type . . . . Le Rhône 9-cyl rotary, 4-cycle
Bore x stroke, mm . . . . . . 112 x 170
Equivalent in . . . . . . 4.41 x 6.69
Displ., cc/cu in 15,077/919.7
Compression ratio 4.83:1
Bhp @ rpm . . . . 112 @ 1200
Torque @ rpm, lb/ft . . 491 @ 1200
Engine weight, lb 323
Carburetion . . . . one Le Rhône
Type fuel required .73 oct. aviation
Fuel tank capacity, gal . .30.0 + 7.0
Oil tank capacity, gal 6.5

INSTRUMENTS & CONTROLS

Instruments: 2600-rpm tachometer, 140-mph airspeed indicator, 20,000-ft altimeter, fuel level gauge, oil pulseometer, magneto switch, ignition (contact) switch.
Controls: stick for aileron and elevator operation, incorporating ignition cut-out and twin machine-gun firing buttons; rudder pedals; hand pump for header tank; gun-charging handle; double control cables to ailerons, elevator and rudder.

POWER TRAIN

Drive . . . . direct
Gears . . . . none
Propeller diameter . . . . . . 8 ft 6 in

ACCOMMODATION

Seating capacity, persons 1
Seat width, in 16.2
Pilot comfort rating (scale of 100):
Pilot 69 inches tall 65
Pilot 72 inches tall 55
Pilot 75 inches tall 50

MISCELLANEOUS

Types available: F.1 fighter with 110-hp Le Rhône and twin Vickers guns as tested; 2F.1 shipboard fighter with 130-hp Clerget or 150-hp BR.1 and one Vickers gun on port side; TF.1 trench strafing fighter with two downward-firing Lewis guns on floor and one forward-firing Lewis gun above wing center section; Home Defense night fighter; 2-seat trainer.

FUSELAGE & WINGS

Fuselage . . . . . . 8-bay wire-braced wooden box-girder with aluminum, plywood & fabric covering.
Wings . . . 2-spar wire-braced wood, fabric-covered. Upper: 3-piece with 10-rib center section and 11-rib outer sections. Lower: 2-piece with 14 ribs each. Ailerons on upper and lower wings.
Turning circle, ft 200
Landing gear . . . . wire-braced steel-tube with centrally-pivoted swinging axles located by shock-cord. Tail skid.
Brakes . . . . none
Wheels . . . . . . fabric-covered wire
Tires . . . . Palmer 700 x 75 mm (equivalent to 3.00-22)

ARMAMENT

Two fixed Vickers machine guns firing through propeller arc by Constantinesco C.C. synchronizing mechanism. 600 rounds per gun. Aldis telescopic sight and ring-and-bead sights.
Optional external racks under fuselage for four 25-lb bombs.

GENERAL

Empty weight, lb 989
Test weight 1204
Gross weight, military load 1408
Wing span, in 336.0
Overall length 224.0
Height 102.0
Wing chord 54.0
Incidence . . . . .2°
Dihedral . . . . . . upper, nil; lower, 5°
Gap at fuselage, in 60.0
Stagger at fuselage 18.0
Wheel track 56.0
Tailplane span 98.5
Propeller clearance, take-off 6.0
Areas, sq ft: Wing 231.0
Ailerons (4) 36.0
Tailplane 14.0
Elevators 10.5
Fin .3.0
Rudder 4.9

CALCULATED DATA

Lb/hp, test wt (power loading) .10.7
Mph/1000 rpm @ max speed . .90.4
Engine revs/mi (108.5 mph) 662

ROAD TEST RESULTS

CLIMB

Time to altitude, min:
0–6500 ft 5:00
0–10,000 ft 8:30
0–15,000 ft 15:45
Service ceiling, ft 21,000
Take-off run, ft (10-knot wind) .150
Landing run, ft (10-knot wind) .175

SPEED

Maximum @ 10,000 ft, mph . .108.5
Maximum @ 15,000 ft, mph . .103.0

FUEL CONSUMPTION

Normal patrol/combat:
Lb fuel/hp/hr. 0.69
Endurance, hrs 2¾
Cruising range; mi:
(100 mph, level flight) 275
Equivalent mpg 9.1

AIRSPEED IND. ERROR

No measurement taken: airspeed relative to ground speed varies according to wind conditions.

CLIMB

altitude, ft

12500
10000
7500
5000
2500

Elapsed time in min

5   10   15   20   25   30   35

APRIL 1967 **69**

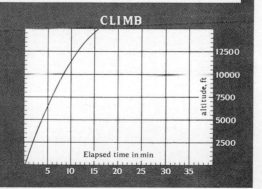

JONATHAN THOMPSON

April 1967

Sopwith Camel F.1 Road Test

At that time, Jon Thompson was the Associate Editor on the staff of R&T, and he composed our whimsical April Fools' test, as well as the sideview drawing for the data panel. Snoopy, of course, came from Peanuts, courtesy of United Feature Syndicate.

GEOFFREY GODDARD

December 1967

Dan Gurney's Eagle-Weslake V-12 at Spa

The racing world was very interested in Gurney's
attempt to build a competitive Grand Prix car,
and longtime Contributing Photographer Goddard
captured the car in all its glory winning the Belgian GP.

RICHARD GEORGE
December 1967
PS
"Does this mean he'd rather be Herb Alpert than President?" Dan Gurney doing something to the Weslake engine.

DEXTER BROWN
March 1967
Survey of the 1966 Grand Prix Season
Brown's imaginative illustration of the frenzy of GP racing provided the lead art for Jonathan Thompson's statistical analysis of the Formula 1 championship.

WM A. MOTTA

January 1969
Laguna Seca— Oh, Didn't It Rain

The Monterey Grand Prix (a Can-Am race) was a slippery affair that proved just right for Canadian driver John Cannon, who won by a mile.

RUSSELL BROCKBANK

January 1969
Around the Bend

The inimitable cartoon stylings of Brockbank were a fixture in R&T for many years. Here he shows a pack of rats showing better judgment than the out-of-control driver.

RICHARD CORSON

June 1969
Nuvolari

A master of illustration, Contributing Artist Corson also had immense knowledge that allowed him to refresh readers' memories with a short story about the legendary driver.

WALTER GOTSCHKE

July 1969

Salon: Alfa P2

The genius of Gotschke captured the Alfa Romeo P2 at Lyon, France, August 3, 1924, when it was victorious in its first-ever race.

GORDON CHITTENDEN

June 1969

Ferrari 250 GT Berlinetta Lusso

For our Classic Road Test, Chittenden's photos captured every contour of this magnificent machine. Many Ferrari fans rate the Lusso as the most beautiful Ferrari ever.

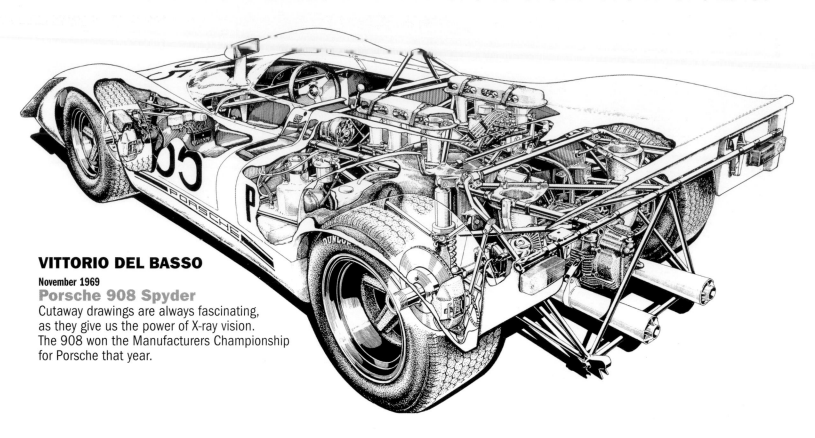

VITTORIO DEL BASSO

November 1969

Porsche 908 Spyder

Cutaway drawings are always fascinating, as they give us the power of X-ray vision. The 908 won the Manufacturers Championship for Porsche that year.

EDWIN INGALLS

December 1969

The Road America Can-Am Race Report

This illustration by Ingalls of the Chaparral 2H driven by John Surtees was the lead for the story, even though it retired after 3 laps.

STROTHER MacMINN

August 1970
Salon: 1935 MG PA Airline Coupé

"Was this the most beautiful MG of all time?" we asked in the subhead to this Salon written and photographed by one of America's leading scholars of design, Strother MacMinn. The photo was taken at the Pebble Beach Concours d'Elegance.

HOWARD SHOEMAKER

November 1970
Sssshhh

Longtime Contributing Artist Shoemaker has delighted us for years with his subtle cartoons. In this one, the damsel in distress feels that she has the upper hand, thanks to Nomex.

BILL WARNER

May 1971

24 Hours of Daytona, Penske Ferrari
"Photographers always look for a new angle for the same old drill. I felt an overhead shot of a pitstop at Daytona would be the new angle I was looking for."

JESSE ALEXANDER

May 1971

Photo Inspiration

This character shot was used to inspire readers
to enter the "*Road & Track* Photography Contest."
It worked: More than 10,000 photos were submitted.

WALTER GOTSCHKE

December 1971

Mercedes-Benz W125s at the 1937 Monaco Grand Prix

Walter Gotschke captured the W125s of Rudi Caracciola and Manfred von Brauchitsch in a perfect moment from the rainy 1937 Monaco GP. The painting was used to illustrate an excerpt from Karl Ludvigsen's book, *The Mercedes-Benz Racing Cars.*

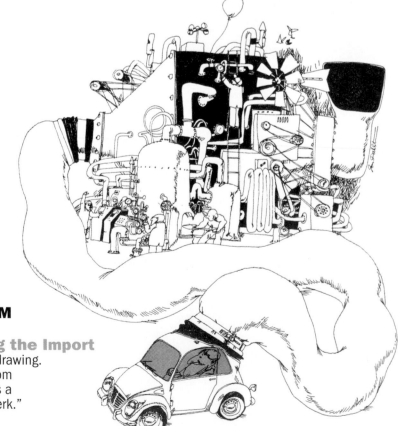

JON DAHLSTROM

June 1971

Air Conditioning the Import

The title explains the drawing. Illustrator Jon Dahlstrom cites his inspiration as a "good idea gone berserk."

The Man Who Fought Sugar Ray

BY JAMES T. CROW

THIS IS A story about a boxer. It's also a story about race car drivers and, in a way, I guess, about all of us.

I'm going to call him Frankie Green. That wasn't his name but maybe he'd be embarrassed to have this story printed for everyone to see and I don't have any right to do that. I met him on an airplane flight across the country years ago when I was still working for Lockheed and didn't have any idea I'd end up as the editor of a magazine about sports cars. I had a window seat and he sat down in the seat on the aisle. He wasn't a big man, not as tall as me, but he was wide, with a big chest, big hands, and a square Irish face that had the thickened eyebrows and slightly out-of-focus nose that sometimes identifies the professional fighter. On his lap he held a thick leather briefcase and this, though he did nothing to attract attention to it, was fastened to his left wrist with a chain. Later, after we became acquainted, he explained that he was a State Department courier and was on his way to Honolulu, Manila and Tokyo. When the stewardess came by, taking orders for drinks, I had a scotch and water and he had coffee.

We were flying in a Constellation, a prop-driven plane that you may not even remember, and a cross-country flight in those days took a long time. A long time. Long enough to hear a man's life story.

What I found interesting about the story Frankie Green told me was not that he lost a fight to Sugar Ray Robinson in a 10-round, over-the-weight, non-championship fight. That wasn't the point at all. What was important, and I'm not certain that I fully understood it at the time, was that from that fight Frankie learned something that was of major significance in his life.

With my encouragement, after we'd settled down and become accustomed to pitching our voices to be heard over the drone of the engines, he told me about his boxing career.

He was from Boston, the oldest son in a large Irish family and as his father was an ex-fighter, it was only natural that Frankie would be interested in boxing. He had gloves on as early as he could remember and by the time he was nine or ten he was participating in the kiddy bouts between the prelims in a local boxing club. In his teens he went into Golden Gloves, got to the finals twice and in his last year in high school, won a Gloves' title in Chicago. He was a fighter, a good fighter. "I knew," he said, "absolutely knew, that one day I was going to be world champion." It was as simple as that.

After high school he went to college for a couple of years, played football on the lightweight team, got his letter in baseball as a sophomore and continued to develop as a boxer. By the time he was 21 he had turned professional and ⟫→

PHIL GARNER
November 1973
PS
Artist Phil Garner's car is the ultimate in space utilization.

DENNIS MERRITT
July 1973
Alfa Romeo, the Romance of Racing
Sometimes all you need is a pen, some ink and a sheet of paper. This drawing holds the spirit, pleasure and freedom of racing.

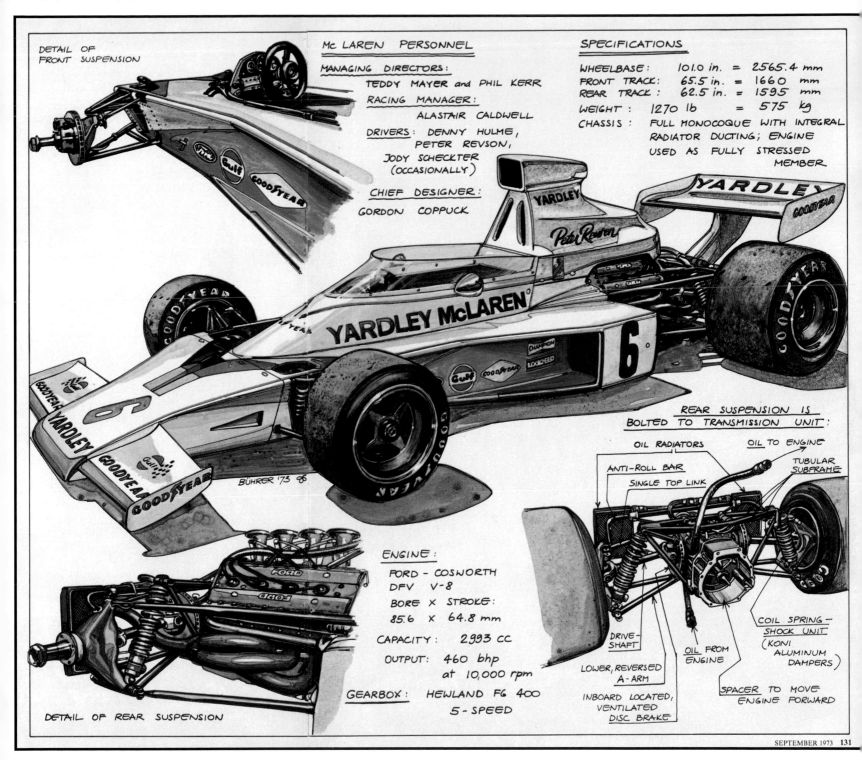

DETAIL OF FRONT SUSPENSION

McLAREN PERSONNEL

MANAGING DIRECTORS:
TEDDY MAYER and PHIL KERR
RACING MANAGER:
ALASTAIR CALDWELL
DRIVERS: DENNY HULME,
PETER REVSON,
JODY SCHECKTER
(OCCASIONALLY)

CHIEF DESIGNER:
GORDON COPPUCK

SPECIFICATIONS

WHEELBASE:	101.0 in.	= 2565.4 mm
FRONT TRACK:	65.5 in.	= 1660 mm
REAR TRACK:	62.5 in.	= 1595 mm
WEIGHT:	1270 lb	= 575 kg

CHASSIS: FULL MONOCOQUE WITH INTEGRAL RADIATOR DUCTING; ENGINE USED AS FULLY STRESSED MEMBER

YARDLEY
Peter Revson
YARDLEY McLAREN
6
CHAMPION
Gulf GOODYEAR
GOODYEAR
YARDLEY GOODYEAR
BÜHRER '73

ENGINE:
FORD - COSWORTH
DFV V-8
BORE × STROKE:
85.6 × 64.8 mm
CAPACITY: 2,993 CC
OUTPUT: 460 bhp
at 10,000 rpm
GEARBOX: HEWLAND FG 400
5 - SPEED

DETAIL OF REAR SUSPENSION

REAR SUSPENSION IS BOLTED TO TRANSMISSION UNIT:

OIL RADIATORS
OIL TO ENGINE
ANTI-ROLL BAR
SINGLE TOP LINK
TUBULAR SUBFRAME
DRIVE-SHAFT
LOWER, REVERSED A-ARM
OIL FROM ENGINE
INBOARD LOCATED, VENTILATED DISC BRAKE
COIL SPRING - SHOCK UNIT (KONI ALUMINUM DAMPERS)
SPACER TO MOVE ENGINE FORWARD

WERNER BUHRER

September 1973
Yardley McLaren M23
Formula 1 Car
Werner's illustration
of Peter Revson's
McLaren-Ford
illuminated the inner
workings of the car.

BOB TRONOLONE

February 1974

International Race of Champions

In October, 1973, 12 of the world's best drivers gathered at Riverside to pilot 12 identical, factory-prepped Porsche Carrera RSRs in a 3-heat event. This was the birth of the International Race of Champions.

RAINER W. SCHLEGELMILCH

February 1974

Jackie Stewart's Tyrrell-Ford

Jackie Stewart became the World Champion in 1969, 1971 and 1973. After his third ascendancy, the Flying Scot announced his retirement from F1.

RICK McBRIDE

June 1974

Los Angeles Auto Expo

Before there ever was a Los Angeles auto show, there was the Auto Expo. Once a year, excited Angelenos were drawn to the L.A. Convention Center to bask in the exotic warmth of European production cars and prototypes like the Pininfarina Modulo displayed here.

RUSSELL BROCKBANK

September 1974

Tailgating and Tow

Some days, it just doesn't pay to get out of Park in the morning.

RUSSELL BROCKBANK

March 1975
Major Upsett
Part of Russell's brilliance is in the number of stories he can tell in a single cartoon cel.

WM A. MOTTA

August 1975
MG TC/EB
Created as a theme painting for the program cover of Newport Art Museum's "The Auto as an Art Form" exhibit, this work used Elaine Bond's MG TC as its model. The painting is now a part of R&T Editor-in-Chief Thos L. Bryant's private collection.

JEFF COHEN

April 1975

Rod & Truck

Look closely at this cover of *Rod & Truck*, R&T's occasional—once every decade or so—stab at self-parody. Now look again. It's Phil Garner up to his amazing automotive tricks. Phil reversed the body on a 1959 Chevy and drove it across the Golden Gate Bridge.

The Brooklyn: America's answer to the urban car?

ROD & TRUCK

ARPIL 1975　　　KU 35p　　SWEEDN KR 3.85 MOMS INKL.　　　ONE DOLLA

BONUS FEATURE: TURN INDICATORS AND HOW THEY WORK

Modern Classic: 1964 Chevrolet Biscayno Business Coupe

VALVE SETTINGS FOR ALL THE 1975s

In Color—The Torque Wrench Through the Ages

The Fairthorpe Electra—Requiescat in Pace

The Garner Car
Direction of Things
to Come?

MICHAEL DORMER

June 1975

Condo-camper

The odd thing is that Michael's architecturally absurd vision no longer seems all that far-fetched in a world of Hummers and self-contained race-team transporters.

BILL WARNER

May 1975

A Day In the Life of...

As twilight approached during the 1975 Daytona 24 Hours, Bill's camera caught the action of the eventual winner, the Peter Gregg/Hurley Haywood Carrera: "No big-deal shot. Just a star filter at sunset. The best racing shots are in the early evening when the lights start to come on."

WALTER GOTSCHKE

September 1975
**Return to the
Mille Miglia**
The action in Walter's
gut-tightening painting
shows Stirling Moss
reining in his Mercedes-
Benz 300SLR on the
way to winning the
1955 Mille Miglia.

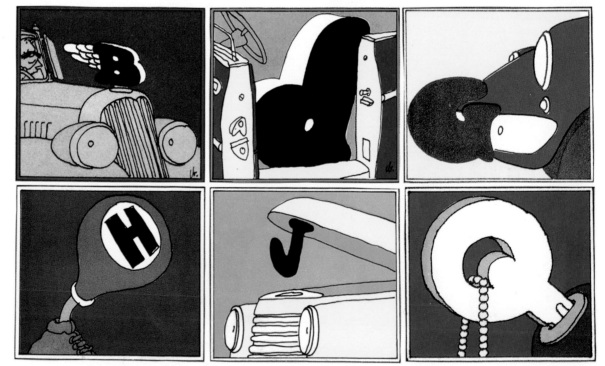

LEO BESTGEN

March 1975 to February 1976
Auto Dictionary Alphabet
Over the period of a year, Leo created his own
automotive alphabet to accompany Engineering
Editor John Dinkel's definitions of technical terms
relating to cars. Decidedly non-technical and
delightfully original, Leo's letters were vintage Bestgen.

RUSSEL

January 1976
Going M
Brockbank's
points out t

HOWARD P. ERICKSON

October 1975
PS
Now *this* is a garage sale...

JOHN LAMM

July 1976
Mass Déjà Vu

At an exhibition race in support of the 1976 U.S. GP in Long Beach, California, Juan Manuel Fangio and Stirling Moss corner side-by-side in vintage Grand Prix cars from Mercedes-Benz and Maserati, respectively, and respectfully. Phil Hill, René Dreyfus, Dan Gurney, Jack Brabham, Carroll Shelby, Maurice Trintignant and Denis Hulme also drove in the event.

JOHN LAMM

May 1976
Ferrari 166 Inter

Of this lovely example of Italian art, Henry Manney wrote: "The delectable little subject of discussion this month is not necessarily the granddaddy of all Ferraris... but worthy of being set in the bedroom just the same while the wifie-poo sleeps in the garage."

EDOUARD MONTAUT

September 1976
Coupe des Voiturettes, 1907
This and six other stunning turn-of-the-century handmade prints by Parisian artist Edouard Montaut—some of the earliest automotive prints in existence—were lent to us by the Briggs Cunningham Automotive Museum.

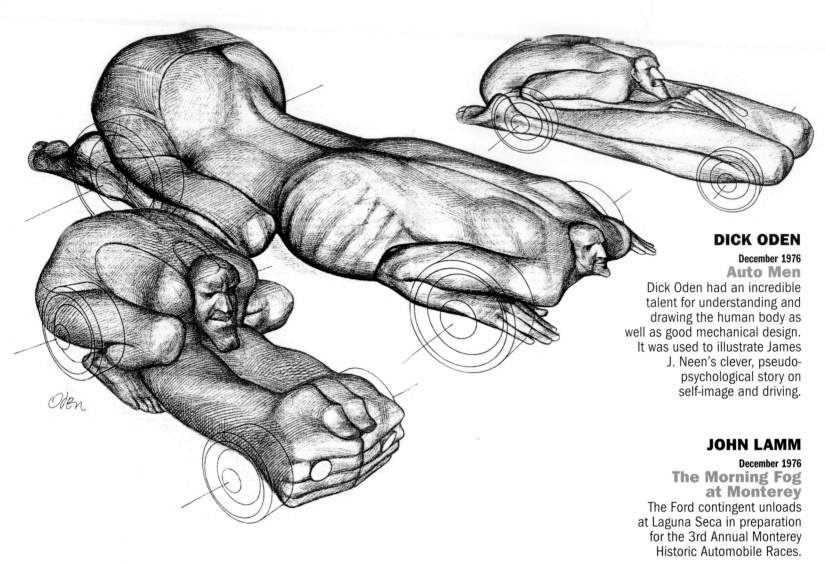

DICK ODEN
December 1976
Auto Men
Dick Oden had an incredible talent for understanding and drawing the human body as well as good mechanical design. It was used to illustrate James J. Neen's clever, pseudo-psychological story on self-image and driving.

JOHN LAMM
December 1976
The Morning Fog at Monterey
The Ford contingent unloads at Laguna Seca in preparation for the 3rd Annual Monterey Historic Automobile Races.

CHAS. ADDAMS

December 1976
Viewing the Remains

In 1976, world-renowned master of the macabre cartoon, Chas. Addams, turned his pen on the 26th Pebble Beach Concours d'Elegance, joining Henry Manney as he dodged plastic champagne corks and covered the event.

REMEMBERING NUVOLARI

ILLUSTRATION BY RICHARD CORSON

Dear Road & Track,

I wanted to do a fond remembrance of
Tazio Nuvolari--a group of drawings
that would cover that magnificent span
of years: the "old man" catnapping in
the pits, the fiery assurance of the
young Tazio on the Indian bike, the
idolatry in the eyes of the small boy.

The Italian is from Nuvolari's grave
marker: "You will travel faster still
upon the highways of heaven."

Hope you like it. Best wishes to all
on the 30th anniversary!

Regards,

DICK

ROAD & TRACK'S
30TH
ANNIVERSARY

"Correrai ancor piu veloce per le vie del cielo"
God be with you. Tazio

Richard Corson

RICHARD CORSON

June 1977
Remembering Nuvolari
Corson's open letter to *Road & Track* says it all about one of the greatest men to ever race a Grand Prix car.

ELLEN GRIESEDIECK

October 1977

Renault Mirages at Le Mans

In the words of Ellen's husband, Sam Posey, who drove on the Renault Mirage team: "A traditional team portrait showing, from left to right, Vern Schuppan, Jean-Pierre Jarier, owner Harley Cluxton, Michel Leclere and me. Harley was telling jokes out of the side of his mouth, Bogart style, but I was feeling subdued, partly due to jet lag and the genuine emotion I felt at being part of a major American Le Mans team."

LE MANS 24 HOURS
No Time To Lose

By Sam Posey

The first requirement for a driver at Le Mans is to appear at Scrutineering at the time his car is there. For each team there is a different appointment time. The cars pass slowly through a dozen checkpoints, being measured, weighed, filled with fuel, emptied of fuel, prodded and poked. Meanwhile, the team's drivers present their medical cards, licenses and insurance papers. Le Mans scrutineering can take more than four hours but the inspectors themselves, glacially formal Frenchmen wearing dark ties and blue suits, seem to relish the tedium.

When everything has been approved, the team is photographed for posterity by a battery of photographers representing publications from all over the world. Our Renault Mirages were posed with French and American flags that symbolized the cooperation between Renault, which made our engines, and our Phoenix-based team. In other contemporary forms of racing commercialism is everything, but at Le Mans no one begrudges you a touch of patriotism....

The demise of the Alpines put the Porsche of Jacky Ickx, Hurley Haywood and Jürgen Barth firmly in the lead. Our Vern Schuppan/Jean-Pierre Jarier Mirage was 2nd, miles behind, but

running so well that I knew I would never be needed as a relief driver, so early in the afternoon I walked up the pits toward the first turn.

Looking back along the track toward the Ford Chicane, I could see the cars popping into sight at random intervals. They seemed to hang there suspended in the distance before crystallizing into a discernible form, a particular car, which then rushed toward me. Only then could I hear the sound of the engine winding through the wide-spaced gears and the long hesitation on the upshift. The cars seemed freed by then of that earlier urgency when tenths of seconds still mattered. Still, as the cars fled up through that first turn, they transmitted to anyone watching them an unmistakable sense of power generated seemingly without effort. As I watched them pass, climbing through the long right turn, I could almost imagine I was still driving in the race. Vividly I could feel how it had been to crest that first hill under the Dunlop bridge and rush steeply down toward the Esses. I could remember how the heavy braking between the earth embankments caused a compression of energy which was released split seconds later as the car catapulted itself along the tiny straight into Tertre Rouge....

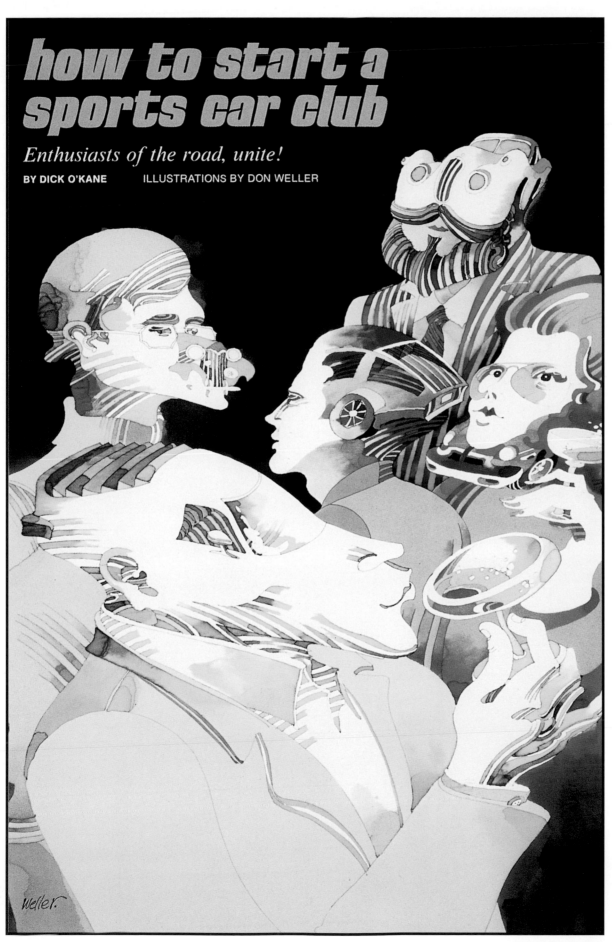

how to start a sports car club

Enthusiasts of the road, unite!

BY DICK O'KANE   ILLUSTRATIONS BY DON WELLER

DON WELLER

December 1977
Car People

"You are what you drive" could have been the title of the artist's pen drawing that was later colored with watercolor dyes. It accompanied Dick O'Kane's informational-yet-lighthearted piece on how to start a sports-car club.

RICHARD CORSON

December 1977
HWM History
In his mini-history of
HWM, author/illustrator
Richard Corson comments
on the origins of the marque,
and on some notable drivers
who positioned themselves
behind HWM steering wheels—
Peter Collins, Louis Chiron,
Prince Bira, Stirling Moss
and our own present-day
European Editor, Paul Frère.

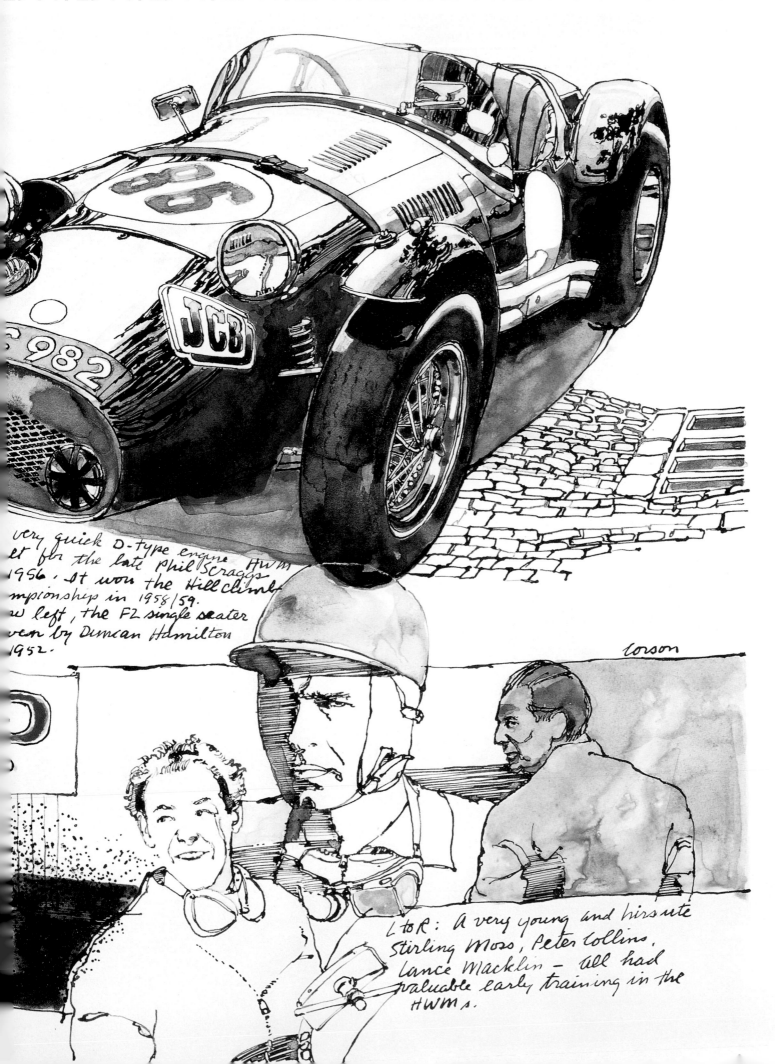

very quick D-type engine HWM
et for the late Phil Scraggs
1956. It won the Hillclimb
mpionship in 1958/59.
w left, the F2 single seater
ven by Duncan Hamilton
1952.

corson

L to R: A very young and hirsute
Stirling Moss, Peter Collins,
Lance Macklin — all had
valuable early training in the
HWMs.

STROTHER MacMINN

June 1978
1924 Rolls-Royce Boattail Silver Ghost

In some collector circles, rebodied classic cars are scorned—not so this impeccable Rolls-Royce with its boattail bodywork, restored by C.L. Bouchard. In the words of then-Contributing Editor John R. Bond, "The Bouchard Rolls-Royce is really in another category; it's so good, so absolutely correct for 1924... It deserves better than 'Non-Authentic!'"

WM A. MOTTA

April 1978
Knight Rider

Our fthfl srvnt Henry N. Manney III risked limb if not life in our April Fools' Road Test of the Quantu-Motion Motoboard, essentially a skateboard powered by a Japanese-made 1.2-bhp 23-cc 2-cycle engine about which Manney surmised, "In a former existence I think it filled some use such as geisha shaper for those interesting hairdos or perhaps a hedge trimmer..."

STAN MOTT
June 1978
Cyclops' Night Out
According to the artist, "This series was inspired by some extremely hairy night drives on Mulholland Drive in my 1958 Porsche Speedster. During the day I drove it sanely around Los Angeles. But at night...on a full moon..."

BARRON STOREY
July 1978
Time & Devices for Keeping Thereof
Says Storey, "This mixed media illustration...represents my usual attempt to combine my interests—in this case, fantasy art, devices, old sports cars and motorcycles."

HENRY WOLF

August 1978

Countach Envy

"This photo was taken in London in front of the Connaught Hotel in the Seventies," says photographer Wolf, who also happens to be one of the finest, most respected designers and magazine art directors in the world. "The English fellow watched in disbelief."

WM A. MOTTA

December 1978

Ferrari 250 GTO

Imagine making your competition debut in a Ferrari 250 GTO. Fantasy? Not for then-Feature Editor John Lamm, who arranged to borrow Steve Earle's car for the 5th running of the Monterey Historic Automobile Races at Laguna Seca Raceway. Motta freezes the excitement and speed.

WM A. MOTTA

December 1978

Mercedes-Benz 300SL

...and from the same event, Motta trades his lens for a paintbrush to present this paddock scene that features a Mercedes-Benz 300SL Gullwing and a Bugatti pedal car, casting the long shadows of late afternoon.

HANK HINTON

December 1978
Mario Andretti
On the eve of becoming
Drivers World Champion,
Mario Andretti is depicted
in this wonderful caricature
drawing, clutching checkered
flags and a victory wreath in
front of Old Glory (for his country)
and the Union Jack (his Lotus 79).

DAVID A. WAHL
April 1979
PS
It's refreshing to see truth in advertising in this PS photo of a lone Squareback in a Volkswagen lot.

GORDON CROSBY
July 1979
1903 Gordon Bennett Trophy Race
Crosby's classical work depicts the 1903 Gordon Bennett Trophy race, with Camille Jenatzy (winner in a hastily prepared 60-bhp Mercedes) sideways in front of Chevalier Rene de Knyff's Panhard.

ELLEN GRIESEDIECK
May 1979
The Red Mist
A firewall's-eye view of Sam Posey for his piece, "A Lap of Lime Rock," where he tried to convey the nuances of driving that track with the help of Ellen's photos. Says Ellen: "The most unusual aspect of this job was that I was trying to take pictures of something I couldn't see or feel for myself—i.e., Sam's view of Lime Rock. For him, a lap at close to 100 mph is an orderly business. For me it is chaos."

Brockbank REMEMBERED

"I think Russell was a lucky person because he brought so much enjoyment to so many people and there aren't many who can say that."
—Eileen Brockbank

By Dean Batchelor

A great friend is no longer with us. And we are the poorer for it. Through his prolific pen and rapier wit, Russell Brockbank brought pleasure and happiness to countless automobile enthusiasts. The illustrations he drew for *The Autocar* (his first sale, in 1930), *Speed* and *The Motor* and, finally, *Road & Track,* are legendary.

"Brock's" reputation was established as one of the finest illustrators—I refuse to call him a cartoonist—in the motoring world. When Brockbank drew a Blower Bentley, you *knew* it was a Blower Bentley. And when he drew a Bugatti, you *knew* if it was a Type 35, 51 or 57. There was no doubt. This ability—a result of thorough research and dedication to his craft—endeared him to motoring enthusiasts throughout the world.

Regular readers of *Motor* and *Road & Track* during the late Sixties and early Seventies know him through his art. I was luckier than most. I knew him, shared drinks, conversation, dinners and travel with him. Even though our association was brief, in terms of time, it was one of the best periods of my life because of that mutual friendship....

RUSSELL BROCKBANK

October 1979
Victory Lap
In our tribute to Russell Brockbank, what could be more fitting than to lead off with one of his priceless cartoons? The caption to this classic read: "In this particular case, it might have been wiser to have the champagne *after* the lap of honor."

JOHN LAMM
October 1979
Cunningham C-4R
Try as he might, Briggs Cunningham was never able to win
Le Mans with the cars that he created—but what cars they were!

WM A. MOTTA

July 1980
PS

Only the eyes are painted on this Shadow Formula 1 nosepiece, photographed at the Long Beach Grand Prix; the rest of this "shadowy" figure is merely a reflection.

STAN CLINTON
November 1980
PS
Mom always knows best.

ELLEN GRIESEDIECK

November 1980
Le Mans

"Le Mans is a photographer's dream," said Ellen in an eclectic showcase of her racing photography. "There are...the contrasts of racing, the countryside, the carnival at the Esses and the people, who are everywhere."

B. STEVEN KOROTKIN
September 1980
PS
A road sign lends a bit of humor to a grave situation.

WM A. MOTTA
August 1980
1938 Morgan 4/4 TT Replica
The essence of the built-for-speed 4/4 TT Replica (speed being a relative term) is captured on canvas by Bill Motta. Its cycle front fenders and minimal windscreen set it apart from a standard 4/4.

PETER HELCK

April 1981
Old 16

John Lamm has captured Peter in his studio at Boston Corners, New York, where he created some of the most famous and inspiring automotive artwork to be done this century. The painting of Old 16 was commissioned by R&T for a Salon feature on the 1906 Locomobile that won the 1908 Vanderbilt Cup race and that Peter owned since 1941. Unfortunately, it was one of the last paintings Peter did before his eyesight started to fail.

ERROL McCARTHY

May 1981
Spurious Signals

Police radar accuracy was questioned by Highway Affairs Analyst John Tomerlin in this feature and by McCarthy's image (right) of a chaotic jumble of vehicles parading in front of a not-so-well-hidden officer, behind the $-sign-painted billboard.

SENTIMENTAL JOURNEYS

Loving thoughts of enchanting companions

BY INNES IRELAND
ILLUSTRATION BY BARRON STOREY

SENTIMENTAL JOURNEYS

Loving thoughts of enchanting companions

She came to me in, shall we say, the late summer of my life although, to be honest, I still felt myself to be a rather irresponsible 25-year-old. She was beautiful, one of the most beautiful creatures I've ever seen. Her shape was...not really sexy...but...sensuous, if you know what I mean. When she moved, she flowed with a graceful charm, this charm being accentuated by her lines curving in...and out...in just the right places. The sensuality she exuded arose from the way she stood...proud, ready to go anywhere, do anything, take anybody on, challenge the fittest with her mettle. And when I touched her, she was like silk.

Her scent was not the exotic aroma of the transparent Parisian social scene but more of a stark, although subtle body odor, heady enough to excite the senses, heighten the anticipation of things to come and impart the feeling that her breeding owed nothing to the nouveau riche. Even to the casual observer she appeared to be an aristocrat, but I *knew* she was, for I had met other members of her family from previous generations and was well aware that her pedigree left nothing to be desired.

When she spoke it was with a cultured voice; to begin, she purred and from then on her tone responded to my mood. Sometimes it was harsh, urgent and angry, but more often rising and falling in a happy, easy, carefree don't-give-a-damn, let's-get-with-it, let's-have-fun, laugh-with-the-world sort of way. She was red. Her name was Ferrari. Her initials GTB....

The dreary motorway takes me past Glasgow almost to Stirling, the exhaust pipes burbling out a fairly subdued rumble as we try to keep within reasonable bounds of the speed limit. But then comes the excitement of the highlands, the road perpetually twisting and turning, climbing and falling as it weaves through the glens and over the moors. Life comes back to both of us as we have to start thinking for ourselves again, and the urgency of getting there for a dram before dinner becomes most imperative. The revs become more precise—6500 for each gear change as we press toward our goal, the exhaust singing out to the lonely red deer and the grouse. Every facet of driving becomes important again—the concentration, the looking ahead, the braking points, the placing of the car for the next corner, the downshifts to steady her, the light but sure and precise feel of the steering wheel and the never-ending fun of going up and down through that delightful gearbox. The absence of other road users imparts the feeling that there can't possibly be any nasty things like radar traps in such magnificent country and there's one stretch—whisper who dares—where I've seen 154 mph on the clock. The excitement of these last few miles, my exhilarated and carefree mood, take me back through the years to the Nürburgring and her ancestors.

As I finally pull up to the castle and switch off I experience a moment of extreme pleasure and satisfaction in the silence, and I savor it before opening the door to clatter over the drawbridge. And I stop to glance back at her beauty which never ceases to fill me with pride, and I could swear she is smiling at me. Climbing the steps that will take me to the enormous log fire and the dram that await me, I reflect briefly on her heritage. Yes, I certainly know where her character comes from: Could it be that I even helped to breed a little of it into her?

BARRON STOREY

December 1981
Enchanting Companion

When a race driver of Innes Ireland's stature shared his inner feelings about "one of the most beautiful creatures" he's ever seen, Storey communicated an emotion understood by enthusiasts.

JOHN LAMM
December 1981
Champions We
When America's only two Drivers World Champions, Phil Hill and Mario Andretti, got together to drive Alfa Romeo Formula 1 cars separated by 30 years, the moment was John's to capture. He did.

Type 10

BUGATTI

TYPE 35

BRESCIA

type 55

TYPE 41 "ROYALE"

Type 57 "Atalante"

MARK STEHRENBERGER
December 1981
Thoroughbred Memories
Mark's art often foretells of automobiles yet to be. Here, for a look back at Ettore Bugatti's work, 100 years after his birth, the artist calls forth spirits of a "Pur Sang" past.

RICHARD M. BARON
March 1982
Speeding By
A blur of blue captures the fury and rush of the F1 scene, as described in James T. Crow's 1981 Grand Prix season review.

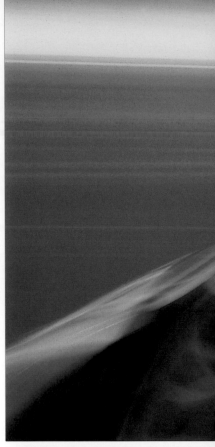

HECTOR LUIS BERGANDI
March 1982
Speeding Past
Ak Miller's Caballo de Hierro, or iron horse, kicks up a cloud of dirt, adding dusty realism to Jim Crow's article on the most famous Carrera Panamericana race winner.

JEFFREY R. ZWART
February 1982
Speeding Ahead
Lamborghini's Countach and Ferrari's Boxer face off in a comparison test. Now, in Jeff's photo we see two old warriors speeding toward an uncertain future.

WM A. MOTTA

May 1982
Roller/Cam
Big car, little girl. This painting adorned our
May 1982 Table of Contents. It shows Bill Motta's
daughter Cameron—then age 5, now age 23—
admiring the magical handiwork of the crew from Crewe.

HECTOR LUIS BERGANDI

April 1982
PS
Héctor's first "fable" painting—
using animals to carry his
symbolism—was inspired by
the angry storms of controversy
in F1 surrounding Colin Chapman's
"double-chassied" 1981 Lotus 88
ground-effects car.

HECTOR LUIS BERGANDI

April 1982
All the World Driving Champions Pull-out Poster
For R&T's 35th Anniversary issue, Héctor detailed the profile
of each year's winning Formula 1 car since 1950—32 in all.

YOSHIHIRO INOMOTO
July 1982
1965 Honda RA 272
Accompanying Phil Hill's Salon of Honda's 1965 RA 272 race car was this detailed cutaway, penned by the hand of the grand master of automotive technical drawings.

DENNIS BROWN
June 1982
Morris Garages
What better car than an MG TC, brushed in subtle tones to remind us of the simple grace of an earlier day? This artwork appeared on the contents page of our 35th Anniversary issue.

WALTER GOTSCHKE

June 1982
Alpine Cruisin'

To illustrate the Porsche 356-1 Salon car in our 35th Anniversary issue, we chose Walter Gotschke, the maestro of capturing cars in motion.

STEVEN TOTH

November 1982
Fred 'n' Ethyl
Everybody still loved Lucy (and bad puns) in 1982, as evidenced by this People & Places cartoon.

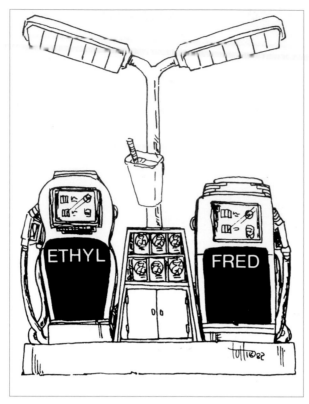

DENNIS BROWN

November 1982
The Great Oldfield-Johnson Contest
In 1910, racist racer Barney Oldfield defeated black heavyweight boxing champ Jack Johnson in a head-to-head match race that carried more symbolic meaning than actual motorsport. Dennis' vibrant illustration was a worthy match for Michael L. Berger's fascinating story.

THE GREAT
OLDFIELD-JOHNSON
CONTEST
Defending the white man's sport
BY MICHAEL L. BERGER

I T IS OCTOBER of 1910. The Philadelphia A's and their manager Connie Mack are basking in the glory of having defeated the Chicago Cubs four games to one in the seventh World Series. Martin Sheridan has just set a world's record in the discus of 142 ft, 2 in. And Barney Oldfield, who had established a world's automobile speed record of 131.724 mph in March, is preparing to meet Jack Johnson, heavyweight boxing champion of the world since 1908, in the new sport of motor racing.

Although an Oldfield-Johnson race could be expected to generate excitement as a Battle of Champions, it soon achieved symbolic social dimensions. Pitting as it did the first black heavyweight champion against the white speed king, the contest was seen by many as a skirmish in the continuing war of racial supremacy. The race was also significant in the development of the emerging sport of motor racing that by 1910 was being organized and systematized by the American Automobile Association. Such a contest, involving the world record holder and a rank amateur, was bound to be viewed by many as a threat to the sport's best interests.

Jack Johnson had won the world's heavyweight boxing championship from Tommy Burns in 1908. But Johnson's status as champion was difficult for white Americans to accept. In an age dominated by "Jim Crow" laws and the belief that blacks should know their place in American society, Jack Johnson broke all the rules and seemed to get away with it. He drank to excess, dressed in flashy clothes, drove expensive cars speedily and recklessly and, worst of all, dated and married white women. In sum, Johnson was increasingly viewed as an affront to white civilization and to everything it supposedly represented.

As a result, the white press did its best to convince former heavyweight champion Jim Jeffries, who had voluntarily retired in 1905, to return to the ring as the "great white hope." Overweight, aging by boxing's standards, and five years removed from his last ring appearance, Jeffries knew that a comeback was ill-advised. Yet he was unwilling "to disappoint the . . . portion of the white race that has been looking to me to defend its athletic superiority." Therefore, he reluctantly agreed to return to fight Johnson in a match scheduled for Independence Day, 1910. The outcome was what might have been expected. Johnson had

little trouble handling the ex-champion, and in the 15th round Jeffries was knocked out for the first time in his career.

Public interest in the sport of boxing suddenly diminished. It was as if many whites hoped to dethrone the champion by ignoring him. Perhaps for this reason Johnson began to explore the possibility of getting into serious motor racing. He had always been attracted to cars, the faster the better, and may have hoped to combine this interest with his considerable physical abilities to achieve success in another sport.

It was later revealed that Johnson had raced in private match contests in southern California during the winter of 1909–1910, and that he had fared well against reputable drivers. It was after these races that Johnson issued his first challenge to Oldfield. But the latter turned him down, according to *The New York Times*, because of his "previous engagements and the objection to racing a colored man."

Although Johnson continued to challenge and even bait Oldfield, the racing champion ignored him. Johnson then dared Oldfield, Ralph de Palma, or George Robertson to meet him in a match race and posted a $5000 bond to that end. In the early fall, Oldfield accepted this challenge, most likely because of the money involved and his lingering bitterness over the outcome of the Johnson-Jeffries fight. Barney and Jim were old drinking buddies. The latter frequently commented on the number of barroom scrapes from which he had extricated the King of Speed. Oldfield, in turn, had accompanied Jeffries on the Colorado fishing trip that followed the boxer's humiliation at the hands of Johnson. Thus, Oldfield may have seen himself as duty-bound to accomplish what his friend had nobly tried, but failed, to do—reestablish the physical superiority of the white race.

Oldfield's willingness to view Jack Johnson as a worthy opponent was not shared by the Contest Board of the American Automobile Association (AAA), the era's primary racing organization. It announced that Oldfield would be disqualified from future AAA-sanctioned races if he actually competed against Johnson. In a related development, the Board revoked the boxer's license to participate in AAA events, claiming that it had been unaware of the identity of the John Arthur Johnson who had applied for the certificate. The official reason given for the revocation was that Johnson's "entrance into the sport would be detrimental to its best interests" because the challenger engaged in boxing, a sport banned in many states, and also was an inexperienced driver.

Although it is difficult to document the real motives for the

ILLUSTRATION BY DENNIS BROWN

Malcolm Campbell held the land speed record nine times with three cars over a period of eleven years, starting in 1924. He took a Sunbeam V12 single overhead cam 18.3-litre 350-bhp engine) pictured here and broke the record twice but the AIAC would not approve them. He subsequently went on to begin his series of successes in 1925 in a Sunbeam at Pendine July 21, 150.76mph/1927 Bluebird Pendine Feb. 4th 174.883/1928 Bluebird Daytona Feb 19th 206.956/1931 Bluebird Daytona Feb 5th 246.09/1932 Bluebird Daytona Feb 24th 253.97/1933 Daytona Feb 22nd 272.46/1935 Bluebird Daytona March 7th 276.82. and finally 1935 Bluebird Bonneville Sept 3rd 301.129.

Ken Dallison 82.

KEN DALLISON
November 1982
Sir Malcolm & the LSR
Ken's lead illustration for Jim Crow's story about Sir Malcolm Campbell's obsession with setting land speed records is one of the finest portraits we've ever had in *Road & Track*. His subject and his loose watercolor style coalesced in a magical work of art.

JOHN LAMM

February 1983

A Parade of Porsches

John Lamm played ringmaster as much as photographer to frame 32 of Porsche's finest at Laguna Seca Raceway for the 1982 Monterey Historic Automobile Races.

DENNIS BROWN

November 1983

A Friend Passes

Dennis Brown's painting for the reflective November Miscellaneous Ramblings column depicted our friend Tony wearing the impish half-grin we'll never forget. His ever-ready line, delivered in a clipped British accent, "Ya know what I mean?" seems ready on his lips. All these years later, we who knew him know what Tony meant.

Tony Hogg 1925-1983

TONY HOGG

I have some very sad news to report. We lost former Editor Tony Hogg to a heart attack on the morning of August 4. The fact that he died in his sleep, apparently suffering no pain, makes the loss no easier for his family, his friends and the many people who had come to know Tony either through working with him or through his writing. Although Tony had a wonderful recall of history, he lived for the moment. Thus, it was very appropriate that a memorial service should be held at the Briggs Cunningham Museum in California, the very place where Tony's much-loved 427 Cobra resides. Following readings by a few of Tony's closest friends, food was served and a band played New Orleans jazz, Tony's favorite music. We feel it was probably just the

JOHN LAMM

February 1983
1937 Mercedes-Benz W125

Peering over a supercharged straight-8 delivering between 550–575 bhp, Phil Hill thunders around a corner at Japan's Suzuka circuit for our February Salon. With considerably more power than chassis technology, cars like these at speed require enormous trust between photographer and driver.

YOSHIHIRO INOMOTO

February 1983
The Cutaway King

Inomoto's cutaways, such as this of the W125 for our February Salon, are the finest of the genre.

1953 Corvette

1961 Corvette

1963 Corvette Sting Ray

1984 Corvette

HECTOR LUIS BERGANDI

March 1983
Corvette Profile Pull-out
For this special Corvette issue (in which we tested the all-new 1984 model), Héctor painted the profiles of 20 of the most significant Corvettes produced since 1953.

148

Glory Days of the Late Straight Eight

Or, they race Buicks, don't they?

BY PETER EGAN
ILLUSTRATION BY JOHN BERKEY

BY THE AGE of 16 I had acquired a desperate need to race cars. Hanging on my bedroom wall was a photo of Phil Hill, the new World Champion, driving a Testa Rossa Ferrari at Sebring. He appeared quite a dashing figure, wearing a white helmet with split-lens goggles and a short-sleeve polo shirt that exposed his tanned, heavily muscled arms. I fancied myself→

JOHN BERKEY

March 1983

Glory Days of the Late Straight Eight

John Berkey depicts Peter Egan's childhood memories of buying a 1951 junkyard Buick with the aim to build it into a race car with pal Ron Binter.

CHARLES GAUTHIER

April 1983
PS

"Cleverly disguised as a racing driver, Bob set off to crash the victory banquet."

RICHARD M. BARON

May 1983

Monterey Images

Perhaps the most compelling aspect of attending the
Monterey Historic Automobile Races is the images it
leaves behind, which are sometimes perfectly captured
on film. One such is this dramatic moment of a 1936
Grand Prix Auto Union Type C thundering out of a turn.

HECTOR LUIS BERGANDI

June 1983
Fangio at the Nürburgring
Our June issue contained a truly memorable 10-page feature with paintings by the remarkable Héctor Bergandi and words from another amazing Argentine, the great Juan Manuel Fangio. Set against eight wonderful images by Bergandi, Fangio recounts his earliest races at the fabled Nürburgring, culminating with his epic 1957 race, which many regard as the sport's finest single moment.

FANGIO AT THE NURBURGRING

26 years after his most memorable race

…As for me, I had to start from letter A. I'd never been here before, and I knew you can't learn 174 bends in almost 23 kilometers overnight. You've got to have a method and the one I tried was to learn the track, section by section. When I concentrated on one of them, I forgot about the rest. It was hard work, but bit by bit the whole thing began to fall into place.

The memory was still here. I sat bemused in the passenger seat as Fangio, who hadn't raced for 25 years at the Ring, kept calling out the type of bend that was coming next, even two or three bends ahead sometimes: "A left-hander now...then down...this one looks like a bitch but at the exit it launches us into a smoother one...now a short straight..."

It came to the point that I had the area from the start to the 13-km post sorted out, and, as for the rest, I wasn't a guidebook but I was sure to have the main dangers fixed in my mind. There were lots of little reference points that triggered reflexes warning me to be careful. Pretty soon I was driving the Alfetta as fast as anybody, but pride comes before the fall and all of a sudden I found myself skating off the road. Luckily the embankment slowed me. Oh, boy, was I mad as hell. I drove into the pit chewing the words with which I would admit I'd bent the 158's tail.

I told my chief mechanic I couldn't use 1st or 2nd gears because of a clutch problem, and he took control of the situation, saying, almost pompously, "Forget it, Juan. Don't worry. Everything'll be okay tomorrow." In spite of everything, I had set up the third fastest practice time and I was in the front row. There were two Ferraris to my right and my teammate Giuseppe Farina on my left. Only three of us had lapped in less than 10 minutes, Ascari and Gonzalez with the Ferraris, and me.

You know, in those days we didn't run a warm-up lap before the start. When the flag dropped you just blasted off into the unknown. Maybe it was sunny at the start and it was raining a couple of miles farther on. The mechanics used to warm up the cars and drive them around the garage area and then push them to the starting line. When they turned them over to us there was always a report. This time it wasn't all that inspiring. "No good, Juan," my mechanic said lugubriously. "Just like yesterday. *Niente da fare.*"

So I had to slam in a gear, get the car moving, and get off, using 3rd and 4th only—at the Nürburgring! Even so I didn't do too badly, and at one stage I led the race for a while. I dropped back when I stopped for fuel, but then the Ferraris had to stop too and I had a new chance to get back into the lead. I really stood on it, trying to pull away from Ascari and Froilán. But it didn't do me much good. The gearshift got harder and harder, and when I tried to get away from the pits after my second fuel stop the engine stalled. After I fell out of contention, Ascari was free to build up a 30-second lead, but even so Froilán could not get by me for 2nd. I guess it wasn't too bad for a first time at the Nürburgring, but I think I could have won that race.

As he spoke, Fangio seemed to grow younger by the minute. He threaded his way swiftly through the Eifel mountains, stopping by the roadside every now and again, remembering some particularly significant spot. He isn't too enthusiastic about talking to kibitzers who don't know motor racing, but when he feels he is on the same wavelength with the listener the

memories start to flow. Even so, Fangio is polite to nonenthusiasts and always seems to be smiling as he talks in that high reedy voice of his, with the faintly singsong Spanish of the people who live in Buenos Aires province.

Fangio always finds a way to be nice to everyone from heads of state to filling station operators without affectation, and without looking up to or down on the person. This is why today Juan Manuel Fangio is the Argentine best known outside his native country, and is a top celebrity in Europe, where, a quarter of a century later, his motor racing successes are remembered vividly. In Germany, for instance, his popularity is astonishing.

I won three German GPs here, one with Mercedes, one with Ferrari and one with Maserati. And the Germans never forget the time I raced with Mercedes; remember this is the only German make that was ever successful in Formula 1. I won two World Championships with Mercedes-Benz and I guess this is something very special to them.

The 1954 race was the first one that I won with the open-wheel Mercedes. After Silverstone I developed a dislike for the fenders of the streamlined model. I remember I kept on knocking down the oil drum markers the *ingleses* used to mark off the airfield circuit. After that race I asked the technical staff to forget the streamliner. I wanted to see where my wheels were going. I also said, sure, maybe inboard brakes are great on the drawing board, but please let me have good old outboard brakes....

Inevitably, our conversation turned to the historic 1957 German Grand Prix. The last GP victory in Fangio's personal record, the race that gave him the 1957 World Championship, his fifth in total and the fourth Championship in a row. Since then, no one has been able to do better than two in a row and three all together. Beyond this, the 1957 German GP is considered The Grand Prix, and perhaps the most intensely fought motor race ever.

It was over 500 km, a distance that a modern GP driver just wouldn't believe. The cars? On the straightaway they were about as fast as today's Coney Island Specials, but the brakes, steering, tires and gearbox were strictly vintage, and ground effects had never been heard of. You had to be tough in those days. Not only because of the distance, but because engines were at the front and all the heat and oil fumes wafted back into the cockpit. Blisters and severe burns were so commonplace that drivers like Fangio usually don't recall them when telling their stories. In the monstrous 1957 German GP, Juan drove one of the best motor races in history to win in 3 hours 30 minutes 38.3 seconds of total inspiration....

Just when I was getting worried, I saw a little red blot far ahead of me. All right, I thought, at least I'll have a chance to fight for 2nd, but I didn't know the other leading Ferrari was just a

few yards ahead. It was when we arrived at the Adenau downslope that I realized the two Ferraris were so close together, and then I said to myself, "This is it! I can catch those two."

I began the hunt, and as we shot past the pits I was breathing down Peter's neck. Hawthorn was only a few yards in front but there were only 2 laps to go! Coming into the North Curve, just after the pits, I tried to take Collins but I overdid it and he was able to stay ahead. His line was better than mine into the next bend and he stayed in 2nd place. But I had the bit between my teeth. I couldn't allow Peter to have the slightest relief, so I put pressure on him everywhere, going flat-out, the throttle pedal welded to the floorboard.

We got into a left-right-left switchback and I moved right beside him coming into a left-hander that had a narrow, little concrete bridge at the end of a blind upslope. Then another downslope and after that you turned sharp right, fast but very, very dodgy. The little bridge was coming at us at a million miles an hour and there we were, side by side, with me tap-dancing on the right shoulder of the road. Theoretically the bridge was just wide enough for both of us to go through together, but how brave can you get?

Finally it was Peter who lifted off at the last moment and I was 2nd. The other Ferrari was right there. It was coming nearer, swaying from side to side as Hawthorn really piled it on. I began to wonder if I was going to get through, but the opportunity came by itself just before Breidscheid, about halfway around the circuit. There were several bends, then a short straight in which we could breathe a bit, and then two bends, a 90-degree left and a sharp right. On the straight, with trees beside and in front of us, and a cliff to our left, Mike went right to take an ideal line when he came to the bend. That was my chance.

I hurled the car into the inside of the bend. I think I must have put two wheels on the grass verge because otherwise the two of us wouldn't have made it through. Mike did a double take when he saw me where he didn't expect me, and he lost the fine edge of his driving for a moment. Well, that's the way it goes. You should *never* let the other guy have the inside of *your* bend.

So I got into the lead and at this moment I really turned it on because I wanted to get clear away as soon as I could to avoid any surprises from the boys behind me. The result was another lap record, a 9:17.4, 8 sec faster than in practice despite the car being as tired as I was.

In the last lap I made sure. I didn't have too much margin to play with, because, of course, Mike was mad as hell and he wasn't about to give anything else away. Nor was I after the hard work I'd put in to get back into the lead. When I got the checkered flag, Hawthorn was just 3 sec away. Well, they say races should be won with as short a lead as possible, don't they?...

JOHN BERKEY

October 1983

A Man Lays Down His Tools

A painter of futuristic scenes, Berkey's art illustrated the tale of an auto mechanic who laments the growing complexity of modern cars, and considers quitting to become an artist.

CRAIG MORNINGSTAR

August 1983

PS

"Bob sat in the doorway, vowing never again to drink from a bottle with no label."

154

DREW MOTTA

October 1983
PS
With age, urology jokes
are one of humor's few
forms that become harder
to hold still for.

ELAINE BOND

November 27, 1924-
April 5, 1984

An era has ended. Elaine Bond, one of the great influences in publishing, and not just automotive publishing, has died of a brain tumor at age 59. Because of the joint efforts of Elaine and John R. Bond, *Road & Track* became the highest quality, and most respected, automotive publication in the United States.

Elaine was a tough lady in a tough business. She was an executive at a time when women in top business positions not only weren't particularly liked, they weren't even tolerated or accepted. And it was made more difficult for Elaine because she was co-publisher of a magazine that often dealt with the Detroit establishment—one of the last bastions of self-appointed male supremacy.

This would have destroyed many women executives, but Elaine was a fighter and the more resistance she met, the harder she fought. Those in our business who thought she had the title of *Road & Track* Advertising Manager and later Business Manager because she was John Bond's wife soon learned the truth. John was the pussy cat, Elaine was the tiger. Together they made up one of the most capable teams in automotive publishing in those halcyon years....—*By Dean Batchelor*

Elaine is gone now, and we can only express our regret that most of you never had a chance to know her. She changed us all with her strength, her directness, her steadying presence: and she and John together seemed an almost invincible natural force.

Elaine was wonderfully astute and dedicated, with an instinctive genius for the business of publishing magazines and a rousing entrepreneurial flair for unorthodox solutions. She engendered floods of anecdotes and memories. Recollections abound regarding her incisive decisions, her unswervable loyalties, her delight over a particularly succulent triumph; and to balance it all out properly, her deep, quiet devotion to John and their children, Marilee and John Jr. Elaine and John moved regularly from home to home during R&T's middle years, and each housewarming included proud visits to the children's quarters.

Somehow we were all part of her family; the staff and the magazine, too. Into the young *Road & Track* she poured boundless waves of emotion and energy, a fervent intermixing of praise and criticism so pure and sincere that it became part of our working environment. We know she loved us all, in a dependable, semi-maternal relationship: issuing comfort, support and direction where and when needed, and fierce, swift protection whenever asked....—*By Dave Black*

DEAN BATCHELOR, DAVE BLACK

June 1984
Elaine Bond
Former *Road & Track* publisher Elaine Bond died in the spring of 1984, and was remembered by Dean Batchelor and Dave Black. The photographer, Scott Malcolm, has captured Elaine's joy at the wheel of her MG TC.

JOHN BERKEY

May 1984
The Breakout of Julio
Tim Blankenhorn's wonderful fiction story about a Grand Prix driver who leaves the track in his car was magically captured by artist Berkey.

A.G. LITTLE

February 1984
PS

For some reason, we never thought to take a car there.

MICHAEL BRODSKY
June 1984
PS
"By wiring the house himself, Bob saved enough money to buy a Buick."

JOHN LAMM
July 1984
R&T's Honda CRX Spyder Project
Automotive restorer and prototype builder Richard Straman converted our CRX from a coupe to a convertible. Lamm's photo embellishes the youthful whimsy of the finished car.

The rally offered a tension between the slick machinery on the one hand and a peasantry having lived so long in the land that the land could absorb with ease the hustling of the crews, cars wailing down through one-lane country roads.

KEN DALLISON

July 1984
Acropolis Rally
Dallison captured
the magic of the
fast modern cars
against the scenic
background of
Greece and
its people.

JO

Aug

19

La

sto

Bu

se

an

MIKE HOLLINGSWORTH

October 1985
1938/46 Delahaye
Type 145
One of only two Henri Chapron-
designed Grand Routier coupes
on the Delahaye V-12 chassis,
this magnificent Salon car was
styled in 1938, but its actual
body construction waited until
1946 and the end of World War II.

HECTOR LUIS BERGANDI

January 1985
One Ford Coming Up
The incredible saga of the delivery
of a 1932 Ford phaeton to the
Maharajah of Nepal is re-created
in this haunting painting
by Héctor Bergandi.

PS

192 ROAD & TRACK

ILLUSTRATION BY HECTOR LUIS BERGANDI

HECTOR LUIS BERGANDI

July 1985
PS

Héctor, at times, liked to use animals to represent
Formula 1's various players. "It's funny," Bergandi
says, "because everyone had different interpretations
for what the animals stood for." This one commemorates
Niki Lauda's championship season after squeezing
past Alain Prost in the points race for the title.
Can you guess which is Niki and which is Alain?

JOHN BERKEY
August 1985
The Genius
A fictional account by
Robert J. Connors of the
greatest modeling genius
the world ever saw. This
illustration by Berkey is one
of the most well-remembered
in our history.

HANK HINTON

June 1986
**A Grand Prix
Charity Shoot**
Hinton's caricature of writer
Innes Ireland matched Innes'
delightful account of the
Grand Prix Mechanics
Challenge at Gleneagles,
Scotland.

HECTOR LUIS BERGANDI

March 1986
100 Years of Mercedes-Benz
A celebration of the centenary of this first carmaker was provided by Héctor Bergandi in a wonderful set of paintings.

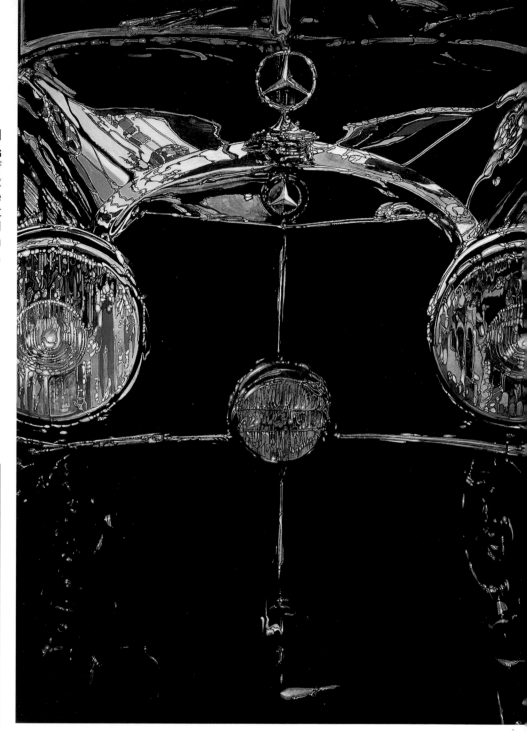

JORGE GARCIA

February 1986
The Ultimate Replicar
A Cadillac with Alfa Romeo underpinnings? What a strange tale.

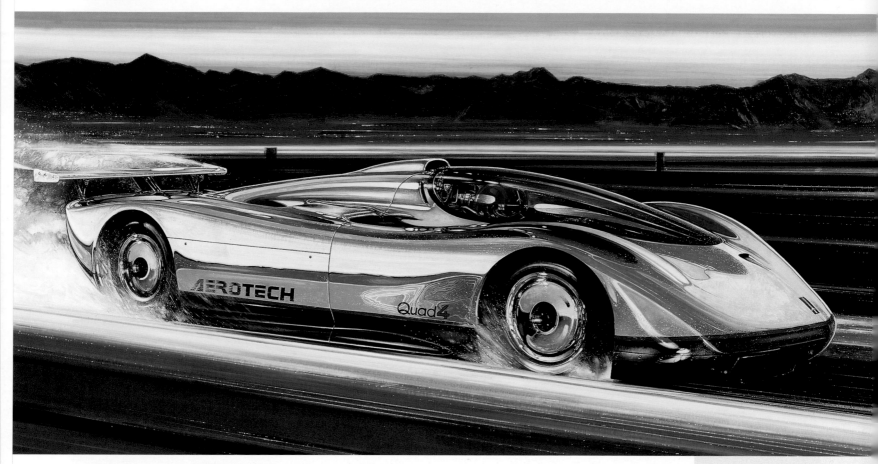

HECTOR LUIS BERGANDI

January 1987

The Aerotech

Héctor's brilliant use of colors brings the Aerotech prototype to life. This car was created to probe the limits of Oldsmobile's Quad 4 engine. "The car," says Ted Louckes, the car's creator, "is capable of doing laps of more than 250 mph [at the Indianapolis Speedway]."

HECTOR LUIS BERGANDI

March 1987

Nigel Mansell

This colorful illustration was one of four that accompanied Rob Walker's driver-ratings story titled "Four Above the Rest." Here, Rob reviewed the personalities and driving styles of four of the best Formula 1 drivers of 1986: Nigel Mansell (depicted here), Nelson Piquet, Alain Prost and Gerhard Berger.

HECTOR LUIS BERGANDI

May 1987
PS

This is another of Héctor's short series of paintings where he used animals to symbolize people in Formula 1. Here the mouse, Alain Prost, manages to lock away the championship over the heavily favored Williams team of Nigel Mansell and Nelson Piquet (the quiet lion in the back).

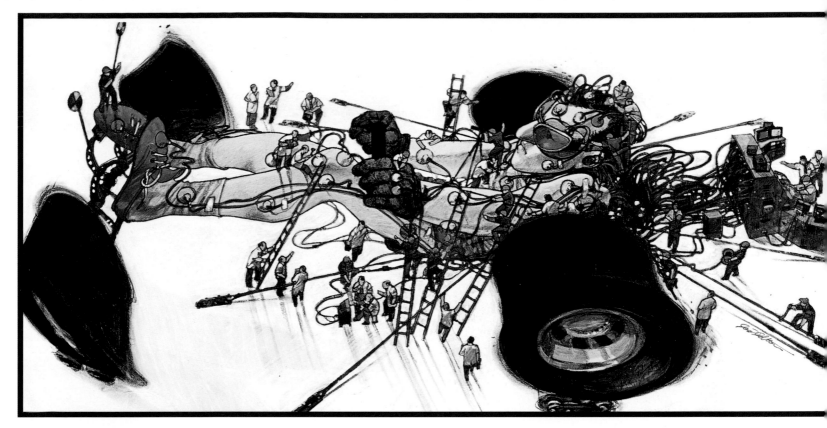

JON DAHLSTROM

June 1987
Fit to Win
Gulliver's Travels may have been on the mind of Jon Dahlstrom when he created this piece for Ted West's feature about doctors who tweaked the driver—not the car—to improve lap times.

MARITTA TAPANAINEN

September 1987
PS
The caption for this PS photo read: "He's not much to look at," Sue Ann told her mom, "but at least he has his own car."

HENRY THOMAS

June 1987

Nauti-Mobile

That's Contributing Artist Phil Garner
behind the wheel of his bizarre creation
called the Nauti-Mobile, a revised
1986 Buick LeSabre created for
those whose motto was:
I'd rather be boating.

HOMER D. CLARK

June 1987
PS
"Bob's life as an assistant race photographer was just one glamorous moment after another."

KEN DALLISON
November 1987
**Rothmans Porsche,
1987 24 Heures du Mans**
This painting of the Rothmans Porsche
at the 1987 24 Hours of Le Mans
showcases Ken's mastery of
the watercolor medium.

LEO BESTGEN/DAVID FRENCH
December 1987
The 10 Best Cars Award
This trophy was presented to the winners
of the 10 Best Cars for 1988. It features
a racing car from the pioneer era specially
cast in bronze in a fine-art foundry from an
original created by Leo Bestgen. The trophy's
walnut base was crafted by David French.

WM A. MOTTA

March 1988
Treed Jaguar
Bill's magnificent Jaguar XK-120, presented from the front in a sylvan setting that makes the car seem cooler than ever.

BILL WARNER

March 1988
PS
"After months of careful aerodynamic research, Bob was able to design a Jaguar E-Type that actually repelled women."

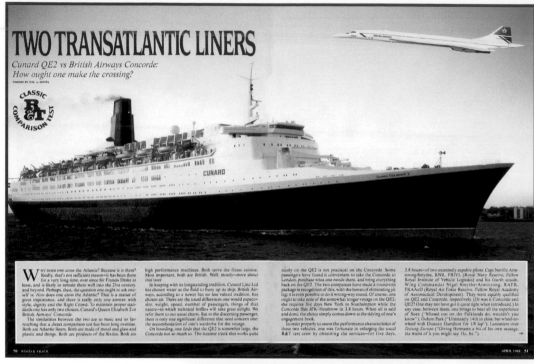

TWO TRANSATLANTIC LINERS

Cunard QE2 vs British Airways Concorde:
How ought one make the crossing?

CLASSIC COMPARISON TEST

WM A. MOTTA

April 1988

Two Transatlantic Liners

Bill Motta was the photographer for our April Fools' Test of the Cunard *Queen Elizabeth 2* and the British Airways Concorde. The total price as tested of the two was nearly $275,000,000!

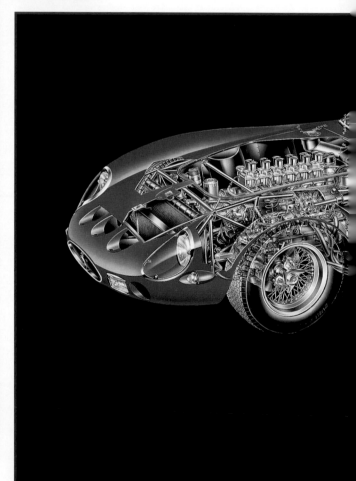

LAWRENCE BRAUN

July 1988

Nuvolari Bronze

Braun's evocative sculpture of the legendary driver Tazio Nuvolari accompanied our Salon on the 1948 Cisitalia 202 SMM Nuvolari.

DAVID KIMBLE

April 1988

Ferrari GTOs

The master of the cutaway, Kimble created a wonderful work showing the ins and outs of the 1962 250 GTO V-12 and the 1987 288 GTO V-8 as part of our 40th anniversary salute to Ferrari.

WM A. MOTTA

July 1988
Cobra Coupe
Bill's glowing style works well with this painting of a Cobra Coupe at the Monterey Historic Automobile Races at Laguna Seca Raceway near Monterey, California.

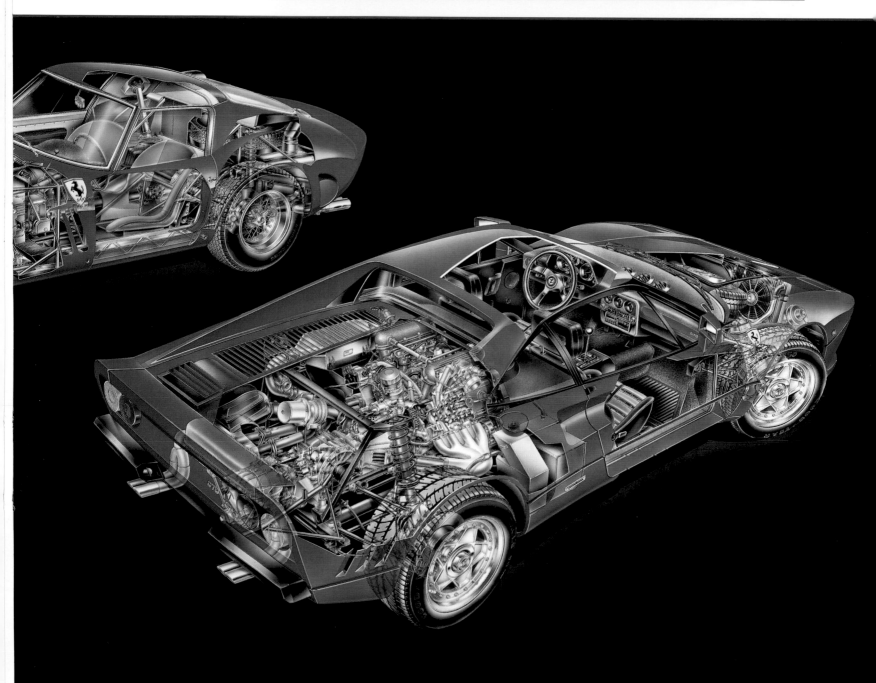

WM A. MOTTA
November 1988
Porsche: Tiny Bubbles
Bill salutes Porsche
on the occasion of
the 25th anniversary
of the 911 model.

JOHN LAMM
July 1988
**Cisitalia 202
SMM Nuvolari**
Sleek and beautiful,
the Cisitalia captured the
imagination of designers
and enthusiasts everywhere.
This one, our Salon car built
in January 1948, had a brief
racing history in Italy.

JOHN BERKEY

May 1989
Road Tripping Circa 2015
How will our roads look in 25 years? Noted science-fiction artist John Berkey provided us with one possibility in this illustration that accompanied Timothy Blankenhorn's look into the future.

HECTOR LUIS BERGANDI

June 1989
Porsche 917
Héctor not only painted but also wrote this feature on Porsche's legendary 917 in a story aptly titled "Remembrances of Things Fast."

JORGE GARCIA

October 1990
The Spirit of Ecstasy

Rolls-Royce's trademark hood ornament is beautifully portrayed in this painting by Garcia, an Argentine protégé of R&T Contributing Artist Héctor Luis Bergandi.

CINDY LEWIS

June 1990
1939 Aero Type 50 Special Roadster

Inspired by the Delahaye 135M roadster, the Type 50 Special represents French curves carried out by a Czechoslovakian company in the flamboyant Thirties.

DE LA MARIA
May 1990
Mercedes on the Mountain
The work of this South American artist is very effective at capturing a sense of speed and the drama of the moment.

STACY DUKES
October 1990
PS
Our caption read,
"Bob's six uncles were all orthodontists."

FRANK & TROISE

May 1990

Nigel Shiftright

This marked the debut of Ol' Nige in the pages of R&T. And it's easy to see why he has since become a permanent fixture.

For all of its state-of-the-art capabilities, however, the predator finds himself boxed in by two lumbering troop carriers.

"What luck!" chortles Shiftright. He throttles down, and, using a smoking Electra 225 for cover, slips to the German's blind side...

Slowly he gains on the trapped VonStockbroker, until, with vengeance in his eyes, he finds himself staring into the Baron's exhaust pipe.

With a quick flip of the safety cover, he exposes the trigger mechanism.

One fiery burst into the startled German's tail is all that's needed.

The Baron's comrades, too far away to help, try frantically to reach their friend.

But meet only silence..

Valves clattering, oil spurting, Von Stockbroker's craft rolls slowly to the right and disappears over the horizon.

A thin, cruel smile of self-satisfaction breaks across the Wing Commander's face.

Shiftright slaps another decal on the aging cockpit...

...and climbs gracefully into the morning sun.

DENNIS BROWN

October 1990
Vintage Ferrari, Vintage Race
Phil Hill never raced in the U.S. GP at Long Beach, but he did compete in a vintage event on the street circuit. Here, Dennis Brown shows Phil in a Ferrari 246, which had been converted into a Tasman car with a 12-cylinder engine.

WM A. MOTTA

September 1990
Testa Rossa at Speed
In this delightful acrylic painting, Bill skillfully distorts the fabulous pontoon-fendered Ferrari to enhance its sense of speed.

WM A. MOTTA

November 1990
L'idea Ferrari
Florence, 1990: "From down on the riverbank those wonderful displays looked like jewelry boxes with exotic little pins in them."

**SUTTON
MOTORSPORT
IMAGES**

July 1991
**Nigel Mansell,
Brazil 1991**
Despite a hard charge
that enabled him to
catch pole-sitter Ayrton
Senna, Nigel Mansell
couldn't pass the Brazil-
ian and eventually spun
out of the race on lap 59
with gearbox problems.
Senna went on to win
the Grand Prix, his
first on home soil.

GEORGE BARTELL
September 1991
Phil Hill, World Champion
On September 10, 1961, Phil Hill became Drivers
World Champion with a win at Monza, a race that
claimed the life of his teammate, Wolfgang von Trips.
To commemorate the 30th anniversary of Phil's
championship season, George Bartell created this
wonderful painting, which we then presented to Phil.

WM A. MOTTA

April 1991
It Benz
At the Pebble Beach concours,
Bill Motta was captivated by
the curvature of this prewar
Mercedes-Benz's exhaust pipes,
as well as the dazzling reflections
bouncing off every shiny surface.

WM A. MOTTA

March 1992
Meadow Brook
Concours d'Elegance
This lovely scene of a mother
and two children admiring
a supercharged prewar
Mercedes-Benz served
as both the official poster
and program cover for the
prestigious Meadow Brook
Concours d'Elegance in 1985.

JOHN LAMM

January 1992
The First Ferrari
It didn't have a Ferrari
badge, but the 815
was Enzo Ferrari's first
car, produced at Auto
Avio Costruzione, his
company established to
primarily manufacture
airplane parts for the
Italian government.

LEO BESTGEN

April 1992
Tribes
In his column, Editor-at-Large
Peter Egan found that members of single-marque car
clubs aren't the oddballs they
are cracked up to be. Here,
Bestgen depicts the environment at an Alfa club meeting.

BILL DOBSON
April 1992
Runyan's Sled Dogs
To capture all 20 of Joe Runyan's sled dogs,
Bill Dobson's drawing ran across three pages!

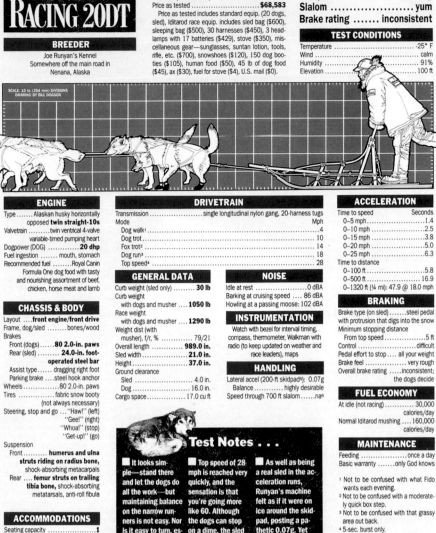

Royal Canin/Amway RUNYAN RACING 20DT

PRICE	
List price, sled only	$1200
Sled with 20 dogs	$65,200

Dogs include 4 lead dogs ($8000 each) and 16 followers ($2000 each).

Price as tested	$68,583

Price as tested includes standard equip. (20 dogs, sled), Iditarod race equip. includes sled bag ($600), sleeping bag ($500), 30 harnesses ($450), 3 head-lamps with 17 batteries ($429), stove ($350), miscellaneous gear—sunglasses, suntan lotion, tools, rifle, etc. ($700), snowshoes ($120), 150 dog booties ($105), human food ($50), 45 lb of dog food ($45), ax ($30), fuel for stove ($4), U.S. mail ($0).

BREEDER
Joe Runyan's Kennel
Somewhere off the main road in
Nenana, Alaska

SCALE: 10 in. (254 mm) DIVISIONS
DRAWING BY BILL DOGSON

0–15 mph	3.8 sec
0–¼ mi	47.9 sec
Top speed	28 mph
Skidpad	0.07g
Slalom	yum
Brake rating	inconsistent

TEST CONDITIONS	
Temperature	-25° F
Wind	calm
Humidity	91%
Elevation	100 ft

ENGINE
Type ...... Alaskan husky horizontally opposed **twin straight-10s**
Valvetrain .... twin ventrical 4-valve variable-timed pumping heart
Dogpower (DOG) .... **20 dhp**
Fuel ingestion .... mouth, stomach
Recommended fuel .... Royal Canin Formula One dog food with tasty and nourishing assortment of beef, chicken, horse meat and lamb

CHASSIS & BODY
Layout .... **front engine/front drive**
Frame, dog/sled .... bones/wood
Brakes
  Front (dogs) ...... **80 2.0-in. paws**
  Rear (sled) .... **24.0-in. foot-operated steel bar**
  Assist type ...... dragging right foot
  Parking brake ..... steel hook anchor
Wheels .... 80 2.0-in. paws
Tires .... fabric snow booty (not always necessary)
Steering, stop and go ... "Haw!" (left)
        "Gee!" (right)
        "Whoa!" (stop)
        "Get-up!" (go)
Suspension
  Front .... **humerus and ulna struts riding on radius bone,** shock-absorbing metacarpals
  Rear .... **femur struts on trailing tibia bone,** shock-absorbing metatarsals, anti-roll fibula

ACCOMMODATIONS
Seating capacity **1**
Head room, f/r .... infinite (watch those branches)
Leg room .... 30.0 in.

DRIVETRAIN
Transmission .... single longitudinal nylon gang, 20-harness tugs

Mode	Mph
Dog walk[1]	4
Dog trot	10
Fox trot[2]	14
Dog run[3]	18
Top speed[4]	28

GENERAL DATA
Curb weight (sled only) .... **30 lb**
Curb weight
  with dogs and musher ... **1050 lb**
Race weight
  with dogs and musher ... **1290 lb**
Weight dist (with
  musher), f/r, % 79/21
Overall length .... **989.0 in.**
Sled width .... **21.0 in.**
Height .... **37.0 in.**
Ground clearance
  Sled .... 4.0 in.
  Dog .... 16.0 in.
Cargo space .... 17.0 cu ft

NOISE
Idle at rest .... 0 dBA
Barking at cruising speed .... 86 dBA
Howling at a passing moose: 102 dBA

INSTRUMENTATION
Watch with bezel for interval timing, compass, thermometer, Walkman with radio (to keep updated on weather and race leaders), maps

HANDLING
Lateral accel (200-ft skidpad[5]): 0.07g
Balance .... highly desirable
Speed through 700 ft slalom ...... na[6]

ACCELERATION

Time to speed	Seconds
0–5 mph	1.4
0–10 mph	2.5
0–15 mph	3.8
0–20 mph	5.0
0–25 mph	6.3

Time to distance	
0–100 ft	5.8
0–500 ft	16.9
0–1320 ft (¼ mi): 47.9 @ 18.0 mph	

BRAKING
Brake type (on sled) .... steel pedal with protrusion that digs into the snow
Minimum stopping distance
  From top speed .... 5 ft
Control .... difficult
Pedal effort to stop .... all your weight
Brake feel .... very rough
Overall brake rating ..... inconsistent; the dogs decide

FUEL ECONOMY
At idle (not racing) .... 30,000 calories/day
Normal Iditarod mushing .... 160,000 calories/day

MAINTENANCE
Feeding .... once a day
Basic warranty .... only God knows

[1] Not to be confused with what Fido wants each evening.
[2] Not to be confused with a moderately quick box step.
[3] Not to be confused with that grassy area out back.
[4] 5-sec. burst only.
[5] It has rarely been better named.
[6] Not available; dogs kept chewing the cones.

Test Notes . . .

☐ It looks simple—stand there and let the dogs do all the work—but maintaining balance on the narrow runners is not easy. Nor is it easy to turn, especially when you're standing on only one foot.

☐ Top speed of 28 mph is reached very quickly, and the sensation is that you're going more like 60. Although the dogs can stop on a dime, the sled can't, so you have to be careful not to ram into the wheel dogs directly in front of you.

☐ As well as being a real sled in the acceleration runs, Runyan's machine felt as if it were on ice around the skidpad, posting a pathetic 0.07g. Yet reactions are quick enough to throw you face-first into a snowdrift.

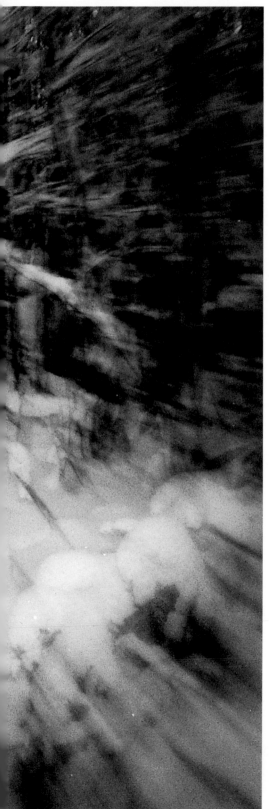

RICHARD M. BARON
April 1992
Runyan Racing Dogsled Team
Unless you're the lead dog, the view never changes.
And Art Director Richard Baron proves it with this photo
taken near Nenana, Alaska. "When it's 30 below,"
notes Baron, "the camera works very slowly."

FRANK & TROISE
May 1992
Great Moments in Automobile History
In their typically wacky way,
Phil Frank and Joe Troise
show how "Gaston Marmotte"
came to be known as
"The Father of Understeer."

· Great Moments in Automobile History ·
June 16, 1910
Chamonix, France
Automobile pioneer Gaston Marmotte achieves lasting fame as "The Father of Understeer."

JOHN LAMM

May 1992
1961 Kimberly Cooper-Climax T-54 Indy
This photo, which is a double exposure, highlights the offset suspension and Coventry Climax powerplant of the first mid-engine car to run at Indy.

LEO BESTGEN

July 1992
Things You Almost Never See
An older gentleman telling a young couple to turn up the heavy metal music? Just one of the many things Peter Egan included in his column.

NATHAN YOUNG

July 1992
Long Way Home
Nathan Young's first sports car was a 1963 MGA like the one depicted here in this evocative scene. Young says this illustration "reflects the joy of driving and the passion of automotive design."

STEPHEN BONESTEEL

November 1992
Stained-glass Art
A few weeks before World War I broke out, this 1914 Mercedes-Benz won the French Grand Prix. Bonesteel has painstakingly re-created the scene in exquisitely detailed stained glass, a medium seldom seen in the pages of R&T.

RON PERRY

August 1992

Shelby Cobra 427 S/C

For this dramatic lead shot of our Shelby Cobra Road Test, Ron Perry told Executive Editor Rich Homan two simple things: To get the car sideways in the exact same spot every time, and to not hit the photographer. Rich accomplished both.

No Fangs

BY BRADA SAVANNE

ILLUSTRATION BY LEO BESTGEN

RED, TWO BROAD white stripes. Chromed rollbar. Fat tires. Mag wheels, or whatever they call them now. Parked on Third Avenue at 26th in Manhattan, Saturday morning in July.

Man leaning on the parking meter beside. Salt-and-pepper hair. Gut bulging from a polo shirt. Clean white tennis shoes.

His eyes had seemed to dismiss me as I approached, grocery sacks in both hands, tote bag, big shoulder bag. Plain Jane in sensible skirt and rolled-up sleeves, old lady shoes, glasses.

I looked to the nameplate above the side fender vent. Clean blank space above "Powered by Ford." On the lip of the front snout: blank. No snake head. No fangs.

Fake. Oops—get insulted someone says that. Replicar. Replica. Whatever.

He seemed surprised to find me stopped. Eyed me carefully. All sorts of nuts in New York.

"Yours?"

A nod.

I looked at the pleated-leather buckets. Neat and prim.

"I knew Ken Miles."

The eyes narrowed. He stood up straighter.

"Dave MacDonald. Richie Ginther." I met his eyes, tried to smile a little. "All dead."

He nodded slowly.

"Saw the first one they rolled off to Ford. Two-sixty. Candy-apple lemon.

Wire wheels."

His lips pushed out together, as if chewing on something, about to spit it out.

Middle-aged lady rattling on, no doubt. Maybe lonely. I judged him to be thinking that. I thought of him in the fake, er, replica, hair flying along a crowded expressway. Probably a curvy babe in that right bucket, next to that polished, pristine red fire extinguisher.

Thought of the bangers patched with sweat and wire to roar at Nassau, Spa, the Ring in Germany. Every dollar, every hope riding for glory. Dents. Cuts. Cracks. Men's lives.

"You wonder what they'd think of this today."

Lady rambling now. Watching a kid on a skateboard rattle by, glancing back at the man, the car, turning to walk home.

LEO BESTGEN

May 1992

No Fangs

Our PS piece—a stream-of-consciousness encounter between a lady recollecting the original Cobra and a man who owns a fake—was brought to life by Leo.

WM A. MOTTA

March 1992

Fangio Memories

Captivated by one of the most famous race cars of all time, Fangio's Mercedes-Benz W196 Grand Prix car, Motta painted its hood with his characteristic reflections.

GUY SPANGENBERG

July 1992

1963 Jaguar Lightweight E-Type Fixed-Head Coupe

We described this Lightweight E-Type Salon car as "a study in gorgeous sculpture. From the magnificent 3.8-liter inline-6 to the beautifully curved head-lamp enclosure, this car is a model of sensual styling." Indeed. And it was fast on the race-track too. Photo was taken at the closed-down Kaiser steel mill in Fontana, now the site of Roger Penske's California Speedway.

HECTOR LUIS BERGANDI

August 1992
The Summer of '67
America was shooting for the moon, A.J. Foyt won Indy
in his own Coyote, Dan Gurney won Spa in his own Eagle,
and together they won Le Mans—in someone else's Ford.
Here, Héctor captures Foyt trailing the turbine car of
Parnelli Jones in the 1967 Indy 500 that A.J. won.

PAUL SCHWARTZ

January 1992
PS
"Signs we hoped
we would never see."

DENNIS HOYT
October 1992
A Poplar Porsche?
Actually, this Porsche 959 isn't made of poplar, it's crafted out of basswood by artist Dennis Hoyt, who needed 4700 individual pieces just to create the taillights.

LIVIO DE MARCHI
June 1992
Wooden 1937 Jaguar
Sculptor de Marchi gives new meaning to the word *barchetta* (Italian for "little boat") with his wooden 1937 Jaguar. What else would you expect from a Venetian who likes to cruise?

JOHN LAMM

March 1993

1939 Delahaye Type 165 Figoni et Falaschi Cabriolet

Artfully flamboyant, this curvy French creation was a showpiece at New York's World Fair in 1939. Following a somewhat sketchy history, it was lovingly restored in time to win its class at the 1992 Pebble Beach Concours d'Elegance.

FRANK & TROISE

August 1993

Miscellaneous Ramblings

From this lighthearted cartoon, one gets the impression that Phil Frank and Joe Troise may once have had a car stolen.

Frank & Troise

Never fails! Take the K-9 unit on a stakeout to catch car thieves and all he does is whine!

STUDIO WORNER

July 1993

PS

"Little did Fangio know that the race's 'purse' was a purely figurative term."

GUY BILLOUT

July 1993

Porsche Faces Life

In the early Nineties, Porsche was losing money—lots of it. For European Editor Paul Frère's analysis of Stuttgart's problems, Billout's illustration shows a crumbling foundation, which fortunately never occurred.

(OVERLEAF)
GUY SPANGENBERG

June 1993

Ferrari 348 Spider

Where better to sample a 348 Spider than a meandering road in Southern California's oak-dotted foothills? Here, Guy Spangenberg perfectly captures the scene with his Nikon.

JEFFREY R. ZWART

December 1993

Lamborghini Countach

When Jeff shot this Countach in 1984, the Lamborghini importer simply handed him the keys and told him to bring the car back when he was done. The result? This simple-yet-strong presentation of the Countach, which is his most-requested stock photo.

DENNIS BROWN
August 1993
Dueling Alfas

This painting of two Alfa P3s racing at Laguna Seca won the Automotive Fine Arts Society's Athena Award at the Pebble Beach concours.

WM A. MOTTA
October 1993
Fangio/Lancia/Ferrari

In 1956, Juan Manuel Fangio drove this Lancia Ferrari to the World Championship. In this Motta painting, note the D50's outrigger fuel tank.

JOHN LAMM

September 1994
Bosley Mk I

Powerful, rakish and purpose-built—adjectives that apply to both the stunning American special, The Bosley Mk I, and the North American P51-D Mustang that owner/air racer Steve Hinton provided John Lamm as a backdrop for our Salon photography.

JOHN LAMM

January 1994
Jaguar XJ13

Intended for Le Mans endurance racing, the sleek, mid-engine XJ13 never saw competition, orphaned because of a rules change limiting displacement. John Lamm captured its beauty on the Monterey Peninsula.

JOHN LAMM

June 1994
**World War II
Jeep MB**

The Jeep played a pivotal role in liberating the beaches of Normandy. John Lamm, through both pictures and words, saluted the trusty military workhorse in a memorable, heartfelt Salon that was published on the 50th anniversary of the D-day assault. The figure hanging from the church commemorates a paratrooper caught there during the battle.

Remembering Innes
By Peter Egan

A few evenings ago we returned home from dinner with our friends Lee and Paula Heggelund. It was one of those bleak nights when autumn is sliding into winter—wind whipping the trees around and rain rattling against the windowpanes like shotgun pellets. We made a large fire in the fireplace, and I began rummaging through the liquor cabinet for something to fight off the common cold. What would people like?

"Scotch," Lee suggested, with the same lack of ambivalence surgeons use on the word "scalpel." Good choice. It was a Scottish kind of night.

My favorite scotch is a very dark single malt from Islay called Lagavulin, which has a smoky, slightly medicinal taste and is good for you. The stuff is hard to find in this country, so I usually stock up on those happy occasions when my work takes me to the British Isles.

On this particular evening, however, I noticed another bottle at the back of the shelf. I set the Lagavulin aside and picked out a nearly empty bottle of Famous Grouse.

I held the label up to the light and said, "This was a favorite scotch of our friend, Innes Ireland. He died last week at his home in England. I bought this bottle six years ago when he visited us, back in California. We should finish it off and drink a toast."

Everyone agreed, and I divided it four ways. "To Innes," we said, holding up our glasses.

I think this was a scene he would have liked.

Barb and I met Innes Ireland relatively late in all of our lives, through my work at R&T. I traveled with him on several story assignments, and we became good friends—possibly because the relationship got off on the right foot.

About nine years ago, when Innes was passing through California on his way back to England after the Australian Grand Prix, we invited him to stay at our home for the weekend.

After dinner one evening we were sitting around talking and soon found ourselves discussing the 1961 Grand Prix season. Innes expressed surprise that I knew anything about it, having been just a kid at the time.

Barb spoke up and said, "Oh, Peter has an entire scrapbook of racing in the early Sixties."

"Really," Innes said. "I'd love to take a look at it."

Barb went out to our garage, dug through some dusty old storage boxes for a while and finally returned with a badly yellowed spiral-bound scrapbook. She handed it to Innes.

He flipped it open at random and there, right in the middle of the page, was a picture of Innes' Lotus 21 flashing across the finish line at Watkins Glen in 1961. Above the picture, in my childish scrawl (exactly the same handwriting I have now), it said "Innes Ireland wins US GP!"

"Oh my..." he said quietly, shaking his head and smiling. "Look at this..."

A good opening page; it was Innes' first and only World Championship win, the first GP victory for Team Lotus and the first running of the U.S. GP at Watkins Glen.

He paged through the scrapbook slowly and spent the rest of the evening pointing out pictures and telling the stories behind them.

Now, if somebody had told me in 1961, when I was a skinny 13-year-old in tennis shoes, that Innes Ireland would someday spend an evening examining the photos and captions I had so laboriously (and crookedly, I noticed) glued into the pages of a scrapbook, I would have been more than a little skeptical. All those hours with the glue and scissors—and bombarding my poor family with Formula 1 facts—redeemed at last.

A few years later, Barb and I traveled to Monaco, where I was to do a first-timer's feature story on the 1988 Monaco GP. Innes and his wife-to-be, Jean, were also there for the weekend, and Innes kindly took me under his wing, showing me the sights and historic spots around the track.

We walked the circuit together, and he pointed out the spot in the Monaco tunnel where, in 1961, he accidentally downshifted his new, backward-pattern ZF gearbox from 3rd to 2nd, rather than upshifting to 4th. The rear wheels locked, the car skewed sideways and climbed the side of the tunnel, Innes was thrown out on the track, and the pieces of his car emerged from the end of the tunnel like "shot from a scattergun." He was seriously injured, but was racing again by midseason.

On the hill leading up to the Casino, he told how his engine had died in the 1960 race and he'd pushed the Lotus to the top of the hill by himself (no outside help was allowed) and damned near expired from the effort. He coasted down the hill on the other side of the Casino but still couldn't bump-start the car, so he pushed it through the tunnel, all the way along the bay and across the line for an official finish.

This story made us both thirsty, so we stopped at Rosie's, a famous old trackside bar. Innes (as I mentioned in the original article) asked for a beer and was served one in a plastic cup. When he asked for a "proper glass," the bartender told him bar glasses were prohibited during race week to prevent spectators from throwing them onto the track.

"I am a former Grand Prix *pilot*," Innes explained patiently, "and I don't throw my beer glass onto the bloody track. You can trust me. Now please fetch me a proper glass."

When the bartender refused, Innes shoved the plastic glass back across the bar and thundered, "Well, we're not paying for the bloody beer." He turned to us and said, "Let's go. This used to be a quality place."

Like most of the better racing drivers I have met, Innes had a powerful impatience for slow thinkers and hidebound lovers of the rule book. He was also, I think, beneath that gracious and civilized exterior, a very tough guy. When he got angry you could watch the color rise in his temples and see exactly why the Romans built Hadrian's Wall to seal off Scotland. He had, in fact, been an officer in the King's Own Scottish Borders and a proud member of the Parachute Regiment during the early Fifties.

Perhaps it paid off. A few years ago, Innes and a companion were attacked by three muggers while strolling one evening on the beaches of Rio while he was in town to cover the Brazilian Grand Prix. There was a scuffle from which the muggers fled with an assortment of head, neck and groin injuries, but Innes' bro-

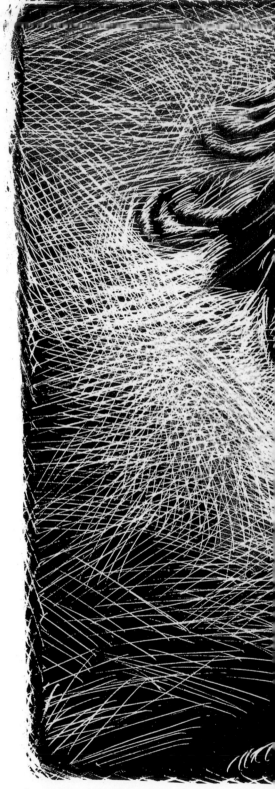

ken wristwatch stayed on his wrist.

"One of those lads," Innes told me later, "will not soon be singing bass in the men's choir."

Then he shook his head sadly and said, "I'm only glad that my old sergeant from the Parachute Regiment is no longer alive. He'd be sadly disappointed in me."

"Why is that?" I asked.

"Because I let them get away," Innes said indignantly. "Twenty years ago I'd have killed all three of them."

Innes always had something of a reputation as a wild man in Formula 1, even in the Fifties,

when drivers were charismatic above all else. He loved a good party and admitted in his wonderfully entertaining autobiography, *All Arms and Elbows,* that this notoriety probably hurt his career.

Colin Chapman, for instance, had bumped him from the Lotus team in favor of the more serious-minded newcomer, Jimmy Clark. This was a disappointment that stayed with Innes, I think, all of his life. He had driven on the Lotus team during the "bad years," when wheels fell off and steering failed. Just when the cars began to win and seemed a little safer, he was fired from the team.

Perhaps it was all for the best. He managed to survive the perilous Sixties as a driver, living on to reveal himself as a superb writer and reporter of the F1 scene, and to become a good friend to so many of us here at R&T. He also remained true to himself and would never have compromised his natural high spirits for the sake of a factory ride, a corporate image or a collective anything. He was a one-off.

I reread Innes' autobiography the other night and ran across a quote about another driver, but he might just as well have been describing him-

LEO BESTGEN

March 1994
Innes Ireland
Leo Bestgen captures the intensity of a sorely missed friend of *Road & Track.*

self. Reflecting on the death of popular American driver Harry Schell at Silverstone in 1960, Innes wrote, "motor racing was robbed of one of its last really colorful characters, a man who thoroughly enjoyed life and raced for the fun of the thing first and foremost."

JEFFREY R. ZWART
December 1994
Dodge Viper RT/10
For his annual automotive calendar, award-winning photographer Jeffrey R. Zwart traveled around the globe in 24 days to photograph 12 cars in the context of their factory birthplaces.

DEAN SIRACUSA

March 1994
1957 Ferrari 250 GT Cabriolet Prototype
A bed of fallen autumn leaves makes a spectacular backdrop for our Salon centerspread of this Pinin Farina-bodied prototype Ferrari.

DEAN SIRACUSA

May 1994
Plymouth Neon
A literal interpretation of Chrysler's new warrior in the subcompact class.

238

RICHARD M. BARON

July 1994

Bugatti EB 110
We celebrated the rebirth of a legendary name with a Road Test of the Bugatti EB 110.

DAVE MAREK

September 1994

Bobby Rahal
A designer for Honda R&D, the artist painted this fish-eye view of Bobby Rahal collecting his thoughts before a race—or perhaps contemplating his impending switch to Mercedes power.

HECTOR LUIS BERGANDI

February 1995
The Hills:
Graham and Damon
The family resemblance is unmistakable between twice-World Champion Graham Hill (1962, 1968) and his son, Damon, 1996 Drivers World Champion.

PIERRE ENGLEBERT

January 1995
Rallye Jaguar
The thrills of driving a Jaguar XK-120 in the Rallye des Alpes are captured by Belgian artist Pierre Englebert. The artist, who shares his last name with a tiremaker, always includes a "Pneu Englebert" sign in his works.

JOHN LAMM

January 1995
World's
Fastest Cars
The Ruf-Porsche 911 BTR is but a red blur as R&T's European Editor Paul Frère rockets past Phil Hill, driving a Ferrari 456 GT.

ELLEN GRIESEDIECK

July 1995

Ford's River Rouge Plant

The toil, sweat and rhythm of turning raw materials into finished cars come out in Ellen Griesedieck's illustration of Ford's River Rouge plant. Husband Sam Posey wrote the accompanying story, "Ballet Mechanique."

JOHN LAMM

June 1995

Cobra Daytona Coupe

The stars and stripes reflect proudly off the left rear flank of our Salon car, the sixth and last Cobra Daytona Coupe.

ERIK RASMUSSEN

December 1995
MG TC

Using an oil painting technique where some of the oil is wiped away to create this special effect, illustrator Erik Rasmussen has beautifully captured the essence of the venerable MG TC.

HIGH-PERFORMANCE DRIVING SECRETS

FASTER THAN THE OTHER GUY

When, where and how did 10 great racing drivers come to recognize it?

We've all had that time of our life, that road and that car. We've all fooled around, probed the limits, learned what a car, our car, could be made to do— and what we were flat unable to pull off. Early on, most of us learned that some other guy might be faster, smoother, able to pull away, even in inferior machinery. But, for a few, it was quite the opposite. Over the past year or so, we asked several of our favorite racing drivers just how it was that they discovered their special talents. Here's what they said:

STIRLING MOSS

"I started racing in hill-climbs, good places to begin because you had no measure except the clock. And when I began, all the established drivers were older, generally back from the war. What's more, there was nothing resembling informal street racing back then, for very few of us owned cars.

"Later, when I drove for HWM, I realized I might be fast. We were racing each weekend in Europe, and the car was so outclassed that the only place I could make up was in the corners. So I practiced outbraking my opponents, using these unstabilizing forces to position the car, and getting on the power sooner at the exits. I remember thinking, 'My God, if I had power like the others, I reckon I'd be running away from them.' "

MICHAEL SCHUMACHER

"I thought I'd be a go-kart driver and nothing else. But in 1987, after I won the European go-kart championship, I got a contract from a kart factory, the Italian manufacturer DAP, to get some money. It was the first time I thought I could be a driver who earns money.

"When I was racing in Group C, I was thinking about Formula 1 already, and I wanted to go for it. Although you can think a lot about it, it is only when you are sitting in an F1 car that you can be sure you are professional. I was driving with Mercedes at the time, the best sports car anyone could be in, and I would have been happy to stay there if I hadn't had the opportunity in F1."

AYRTON SENNA

"It's difficult to say. I think when I started running well in international go-kart races I dreamed about driving single-seaters—but I didn't know what it would be like. Then, when I had the opportunity to drive a single-seater and be quick and win races, I realized there was no magic about it. And that it was also perhaps possible to one day become a competitive Formula 1 driver.

"In Formula Ford racing I realized it truly was achievable. It would be difficult, I knew, but I had some hope and belief that if I could develop myself and carry on with a good team and good cars, I could develop myself into an F1 driver." →

May 1995
Faster Than The Other Guy

When was that moment of inspiration, that epiphany, when 10 great drivers knew they had what it takes? We asked; they revealed.

RON PERRY
April 1995
Rain-soaked Jaguar
What could be more evocative of England than a Jaguar XJR caught in the middle of a downpour? Photographer Ron Perry uses water droplets to great effect here.

NIGEL SNOWDON
September 1995
Ferrari Flight
Ferrari driver Gerhard Berger gives new meaning to the term, "flying start" at the Monaco Grand Prix.

199

BERNARD CAHIER

June 1995

Fangio and Collins at the Nürburgring, 1956

"My portraits of Fangio/Collins clearly show the drivers' tension before a tough Grand Prix, which, in these days, lasted 3½ hours! Fangio was very fond of Peter Collins and Peter, who was beloved by Ferrari, had an immense respect and admiration for Fangio. Peter, a true gentleman, proved this in a magnificent way when, at the 1956 Italian GP in Monza, he voluntarily gave his car to Fangio who had retired. You could share a car and the points at that epoch. The result was that Fangio won on that occasion of his fourth World Championship title, and never forgot Collins' noble gesture. Collins told me later on that he was just too young for the responsibility of being World Champion and that Fangio really deserved it anyway! (Would you believe that today!)"

BERNARD CAHIER

June 1995

Targa Florio, 1955

"The last round of the 1955 Sports Car Championship season took place on the romantic and ever prestigious Targa Florio circuit near Palermo. It was there that the mighty Mercedes team had to beat the Ferraris for the title! The difference between the two teams was striking. On one side, the 300SLRs with one hundred mechanics, Fangio, Collins, Fitch, etc.... On the other side, a dozen brave Italians to look after the Ferrari of Castellotti/Manzon! The race was fantastic all the way! Moss went off deep into a field only to be brought back onto the road by wild Sicilians. Later on, thanks to his brilliant co-driver Peter Collins, they won the race and the title! Castellotti/Manzon fought bravely and when in 2nd place, on the last lap of the race, Manzon had a flat tire, he changed it himself and still finished in a remarkable 3rd place."

BARRY ROWE

November 1995

Alfa Romeo 8C 2900 B

In this scene from the 1938 Mille Miglia, English artist Barry Rowe depicts Clemente Biondetti at the wheel of the winning Alfa Romeo 8C 2900 B, closely pursued by teammate Carlo Pinacuda.

HECTOR LUIS BERGANDI

October 1995

Juan Manuel Fangio

A masterful depiction of the greatest Grand Prix driver ever, five-time World Champion Juan Manuel Fangio. Bergandi manages to capture the man's grace, determination and stoicism.

MAJOR ELLIOTT C. TOURS

June 1996

"But Officer..."

"Do you have *any* idea of how fast you were going?" read the PS photo caption of Eugenio Castellotti in the Lancia-Ferrari, seemingly being interrogated by uniformed men at the Nürburgring, 1956.

DAVID GROVE

May 1996

When The Wall Came Down

A car can define chapters of our lives, as this Mazda 626 did for author Ed Serotta in his piece, "When the War was Cold and the Car had Hubcaps." Grove's haunting work captures the essence of Serotta's personal diary on the fall of Communism.

BARRY ROWE

April 1996
Scene from Brooklands

One of the best-dressed crowds in racing history is frozen in time by British artist Barry Rowe.

D. MAYNARDO KREMILLER

May 1996
Joyride

The artist wrote that he has enjoyed *Road & Track* for many years, but that the *Road* part outweighs the *Track*. So he created this sculpture titled "Joyride, the 2015 Steamster."

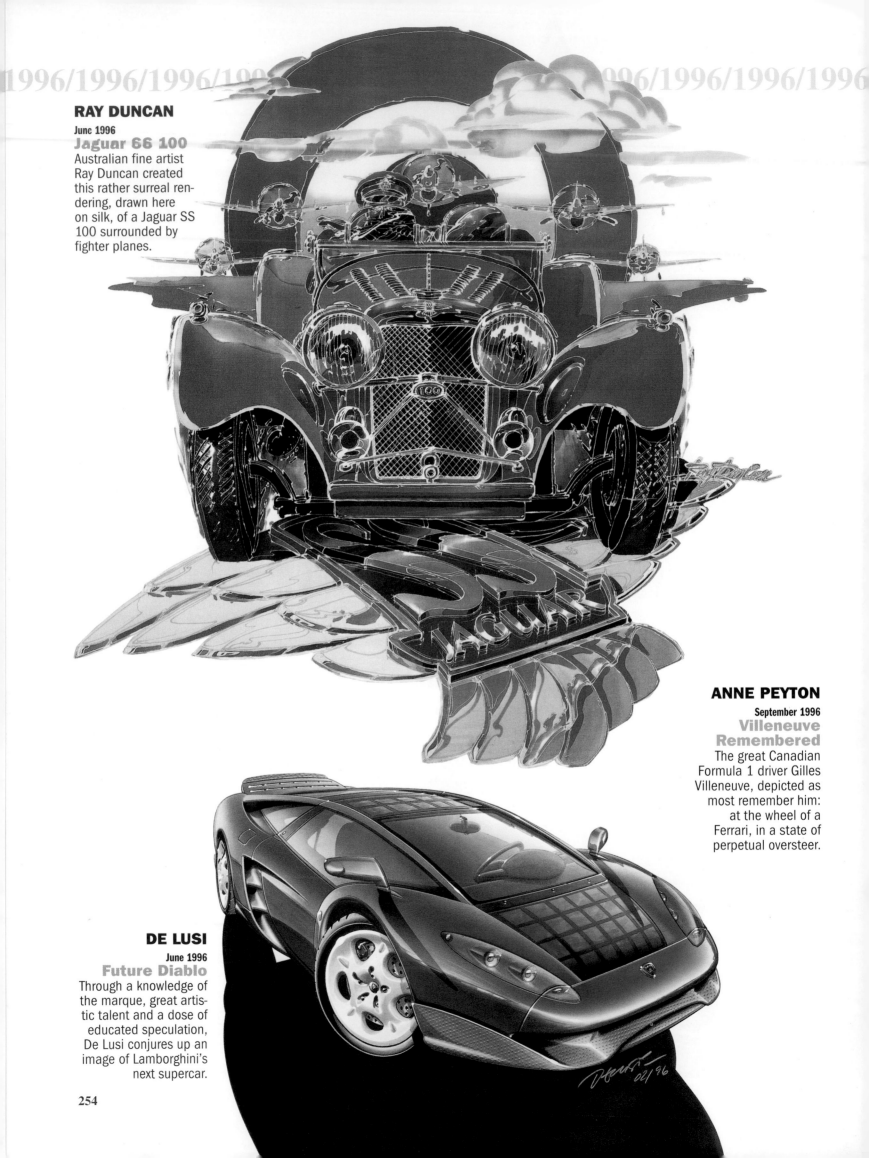

RAY DUNCAN

June 1996
Jaguar SS 100
Australian fine artist Ray Duncan created this rather surreal rendering, drawn here on silk, of a Jaguar SS 100 surrounded by fighter planes.

ANNE PEYTON

September 1996
Villeneuve Remembered
The great Canadian Formula 1 driver Gilles Villeneuve, depicted as most remember him: at the wheel of a Ferrari, in a state of perpetual oversteer.

DE LUSI

June 1996
Future Diablo
Through a knowledge of the marque, great artistic talent and a dose of educated speculation, De Lusi conjures up an image of Lamborghini's next supercar.

254

RICHARD M. BARON
September 1996
Slumbering D-Types
R&T Art Director and Jaguar aficionado Richard M. Baron braved the chill morning air to capture these dormant racing legends before heading to the Le Mans circuit.

RON PERRY
August 1996
Stealth Wheel
There's a near-abstract quality to this one, reflections of flowers in the chrome-plated wheel of a Dodge Stealth. Narrow depth of field is used to great advantage.

SCALE: 10 in.(254mm) DIVISIONS
DRAWING BY BILL DOBSON

BILL DOBSON

November 1996
Jaguar XK8 Sideview
A phantom view of Jaguar's latest by Bill Dobson, whose meticulous sideview drawings have been gracing *Road & Track's* data panels for 20 years.

WM A. MOTTA

September 1996
Porsche 917/30
The fury of the world-beating Porsche 917/30 that dominated Can-Am racing in the early Seventies comes alive through Wm A. Motta's acrylic-on-canvas work.

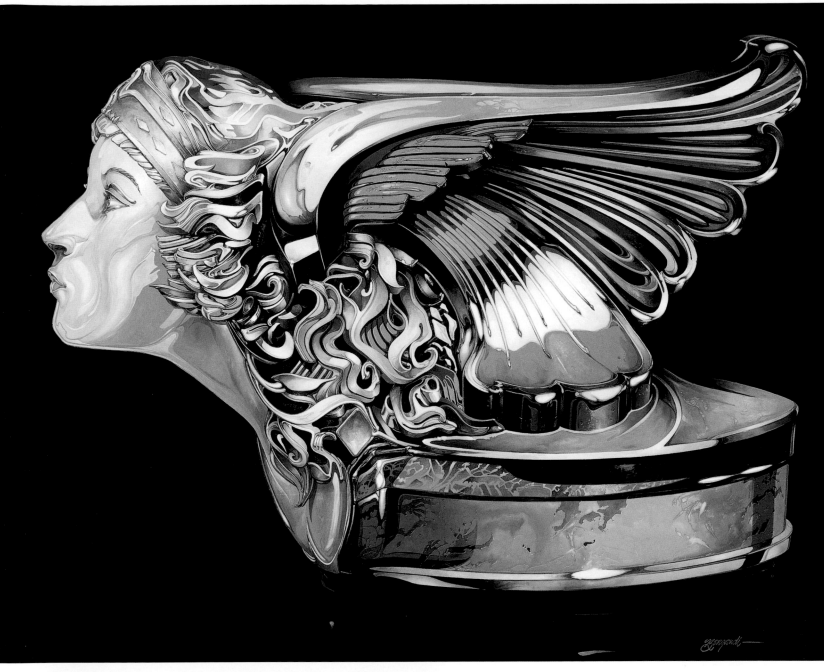

HECTOR LUIS BERGANDI

August 1996
Buick Hood Ornament
"When I was a kid, my attention was captured by the hood ornament of a 1926 Buick... Not long ago, I saw a photograph of such a car. The ornament was no more than a few millimeters high in the photo, but it brought it all back. This painting grew from the idealized memory."

DAVE KURZ

April 1996
Bugatti Coupe
A photo? No, it's a photo-realistic painting done with pastels on sandpaper by artist Dave Kurz of an elegant Bugatti coupe rumored to be the prototype for the famed Atlantic Coupe.

Al Jr. said to the boy—in that easy relaxed way that all great Daddies have,

BARRON STOREY

December 1996

Al Unser Jr.

Somehow, Barron Storey's montage of Al Unser Jr. captures both his intensity and his easygoing nature in a fine ode to a former Indy Car champion who struggled in 1996 with a less-than-competitive car.

WM A. MOTTA

November 1996

Memories

Exactly what is the old gent thinking as he contemplates the aft end of this 1946 Cadillac in this work titled "Memories"? The reflections here are far more involved than the ones that play off the chrome surface of a bumper.

JAMES CRAWFORD

December 1996

Santa Claus: Car Guy

Santa, or perhaps a nontraditional version as *Road & Track* readers
might picture him, wishes all a Merry Christmas from our PS page—
and another 50 years of enjoyment from the art of our magazine.

INDEX/INDEX/INDEX/INDEX/INDEX/INDEX/INDEX/IN

50 YEARS OF ROAD & TRACK

THE ART OF THE AUTOMOBILE